AN ATLAS OF RUSSIAN HISTORY

Eleven Centuries of Changing Borders

AN ATLAS OF RUSSIAN HISTORY

Eleven Centuries of Changing Borders

by ALLEN F. CHEW

Revised Edition

NEW HAVEN AND LONDON, YALE UNIVERSITY PRESS, 1970

Contents

Preface to Revised Edition

The differences between the original and the revised editions of this atlas are mainly of three types:

1. Additions, including maps depicting geographic features and an appendix of cross-referenced place name changes. The additional maps were adapted from data in:

Geograficheskiy Atlas Dlya Uchiteley Sredney Shkoly, ed. Yu. V. Filippov et al. Moscow, 1954 and *Atlas SSSR,* ed. A. N. Baranov et al. 2d ed. Moscow, 1969.

2. More precise information on present boundaries, based on the excellent series of pamphlets issued by The Geographer, U.S. Department of State, under the general title *International Boundary Study . . .*

3. Technical improvements in many of the maps for increased legibility.

There are minor additions to a few maps and texts which are directly attributable to the welcome response to my request for suggestions. I wish to thank all who were kind enough to forward their comments. I am especially indebted to C. Ian Jackson for bringing to my attention the lease of part of the Alaskan panhandle (see Map 26) and to Donald G. Janelle for constructively criticizing the draft of the texts which accompany Maps 35–37.

Thanks are also due Henry J. Armani for suggesting the use of dual dates for the annexation of the western Georgian states. In this regard an additional caveat concerning the term "annexation" is in order. Not only in relation to remote areas (as noted in the preface to the first edition), but even when applied to the heart of Muscovy, that word may be misleading. Frequently a period of vassalage or a protectorate status preceded formal incorporation into the state. The reader should note, beginning with Map 8, that not all of these nuances have been mentioned and that "annexation" is not necessarily used in a de jure sense.

ALLEN F. CHEW

Colorado Springs
April 1970

Preface

The maps in this atlas depict, generally in chronological order, the important changes in Russia's boundaries and possessions from the formation of the embryonic state of Kievan Rus in the ninth century to the most recent revisions resulting from the Second World War. The text describes salient features of these changes. The underlying causes, the concomitant defensive and—more often—offensive wars, and the significant results of the changes constitute much of the drama of Russian history. A full narration is obviously beyond the scope of an atlas, which is intended to supplement the more comprehensive histories that tell the complex story behind a nation's moving frontiers.

The reader is asked not to concern himself with the semantic niceties of the designation "Russia," which is often the object of dispute. Merely as a matter of convenience, the term "Russia" has been applied here to all areas under the political control of the central government, whether it be Kievan Rus, Muscovy, the Tsarist Empire, or the Soviet Union.

The dates of Russia's acquisition of certain remote regions are obscure; this is notably true of some of the Arctic islands, northeastern Siberia, and Finland prior to the fourteenth century. Certainly the early Novgorodian fur traders did not habitually "implant the flag" to demarcate their domains in the vast Finnish wilderness, and neither did the Cossack adventurers in northeastern Siberia. Even when Russian explorers did bury plaques to substantiate territorial claims, there is reason to question the dates inscribed on some of them. Consequently, different authors cite varying dates for the "annexation" of Chukotka, for one example; even fairly reliable Soviet sources give conflicting dates for that area. I have tried to avoid such arbitrary and misleading dates by noting approximately when these areas were first explored or exploited by Russians; their "annexation" was often an evolutionary, informal, and piecemeal process.

Maps 1–3, covering the early tenth to the mid-eleventh centuries, include most of the Russian cities and towns known to have existed during those times, as verified by recent archaeology and historiography. Those shown on Map 4 (1054–1237 A.D.) were similarly confirmed, but by then they were already too numerous to depict in their entirety on maps of this scale. For subsequent periods, when there is no longer anything remarkable about the proliferation of urban centers, only major towns or those particularly pertinent to the period and topic covered by the map have been included.

It should be noted that the determination of the "left" and "right" banks of rivers—which so frequently serve as boundaries—is made while facing downstream.

The transliteration system is a modification of that employed by the Library of Congress, slightly simplified for convenience. Accents are omitted, and while personal names ending in *skiy* are rendered by the more familiar *sky,* place names ending in *skiy* are merely shortened to *ski.* In general, the ending *iy* is rendered *i* (Vasil*i*, Velik*i*, Nizhn*i*, etc.).

For the section relating to Russia's North American possessions, the forms are those usually employed by American geographers, e.g. Baranof (instead of Baranov) Island. Deviations have also been made in the case of certain very familiar place names: for example, the city of Moskva is designated by its common English-language name, Moscow, and the Dnestr and Dnepr rivers are rendered by the more familiar forms Dniester and Dnieper. Because this atlas is intended to depict Russia's history, the Russian spelling has been favored for places of varying or disputed nationality, e.g. Lvov instead of Lwow.

If the sources for the hundreds of specific facts condensed in this brief atlas were all cited, the documentation would exceed the text in length. The author, incidental to teaching Russian history over a period of five years, collected pertinent notes from scores of publications, both Western and Soviet. Although no sources were accepted without evaluation and cross-checking, certain ones proved especially valuable. Among these were:

Atlas Istorii Geograficheskikh Otkrytiy i Issledovaniy, ed. K. A. Salishchev et al. Moscow, 1959
Bazilevich, K. V., et al., *Atlas Istorii SSSR.* 3 vols. Moscow, 1959
Bolshaya Sovetskaya Entsiklopediya. 2d ed. Moscow, 1949–57
Grekov, B. D., et al., *Ocherki Istorii SSSR.* Vol. 1 (9th–13th centuries). Moscow, 1953

x

Kratkaya Geograficheskaya Entsiklopediya, chief ed. A. A. Grigorev. 5 vols. Moscow, 1960–66

Tikhomirov, M., *The Towns of Ancient Rus,* trans. Y. Sdobnikov. Moscow, 1959

Vernadsky, George, *Ancient Russia.* New Haven, Yale University Press, 1943

——, *Kievan Russia.* New Haven, Yale University Press, 1948

——, *The Mongols and Russia.* New Haven, Yale University Press, 1953

——, *Russia at the Dawn of the Modern Age.* New Haven, Yale University Press, 1959

I wish to express my sincere thanks to my colleagues, Victor D. Sutch (historian) for reading the entire manuscript and offering constructive criticism; William M. Roberts (geographer) for technical advice; and Richard F. Rosser (political scientist) for verifying portions of the text. I am also indebted to Donald E. Jacobs for his excellent technical assistance with the maps, although the responsibility for their historical accuracy is mine alone. Finally, this laborious project would not have been completed without the patient secretarial services of my wife, Irene.

To the valid but stereotyped comment that any errors are the responsibility of the author, I wish to add that I would appreciate suggestions for any factual corrections which may be appropriate.

ALLEN F. CHEW

Colorado Springs
October 1966

AN ATLAS OF RUSSIAN HISTORY

Eleven Centuries of Changing Borders

Map 1. Russia in the Time of Oleg, c. 878–912 A.D.

The Founding of the Russian State

The history of Russia as an organized state is traditionally considered to begin with the "coming of the Varangians," led by the semi-legendary Rurik, in the latter half of the ninth century (c. 856–62 A.D.). There had been earlier incursions by Norse merchant warriors into what later came to be known as European Russia, where they had encountered numerous small river settlements and larger city-states inhabited by the several independent eastern Slavic tribes. It was only when the Varangians came in force to settle permanently that these Slavic tribes achieved the tenuous unity of a loose federation, known in modern historiography as Kievan Rus.

The Norsemen, who had been originally based at Novgorod, close to the Baltic terminus of the trade routes to Constantinople and the Near East, soon established their capital at the more strategically located city of Kiev (c. 878–82). The first independent Varangian ruler of Kievan Rus, Oleg, was concerned with the protection of commercially vital waterways against the threat from the east, in this case the competition of the Khazars. The problem of the defense of the southeastern frontier, the unobstructed steppe zone, remained a recurring theme in Russian history for centuries to come; it was ultimately resolved by the annexation of the steppes.

Oleg initiated the Russian policy of expansion and annexation. By the time of his death (c. 912) he ruled a large realm (Map 1) which included a majority of the eastern Slavic tribes.

RUSSIA IN THE TIME OF OLEG, C. 878–912 A.D.

MAP I

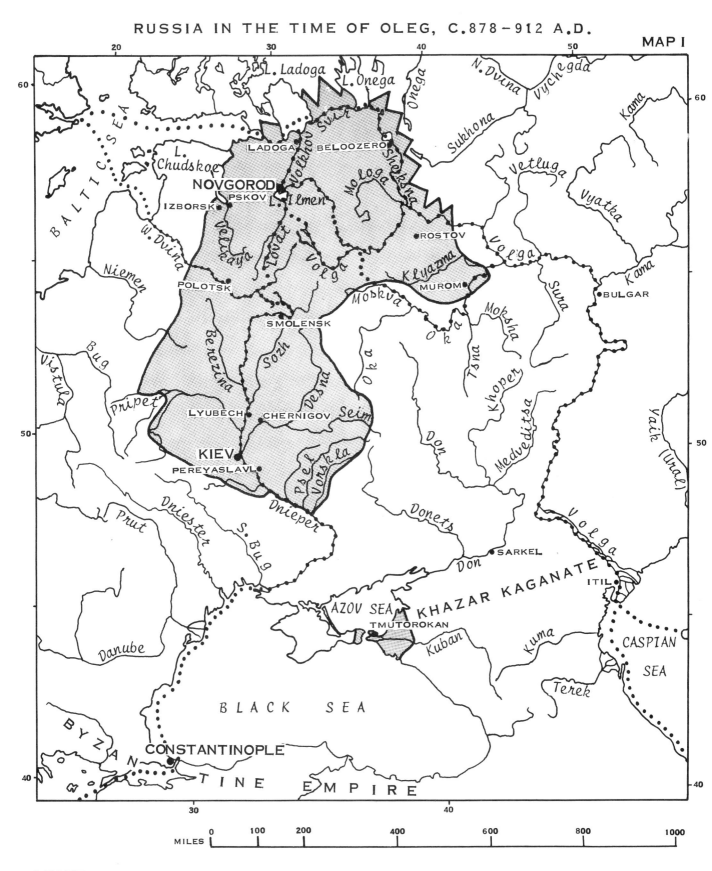

LEGEND •••••• MAIN TRADE ROUTES

▨ RUSSIA C. 912

MILES 0 100 200 400 600 800 1000

Map 2. Russia in the Time of Igor (c. 912–945) and Svyatoslav (945–972)

The First "Russian Empire"

Oleg's successor, Igor, made few permanent gains; his reign was beset with internal revolts, the first serious incursions of the steppe nomads (the Pechenegs, or Patzinaks), and generally unsuccessful foreign campaigns. At his death in 945, his widow, Olga, served as regent for their infant son, Svyatoslav. During the brief span of Svyatoslav's active rule (c. 962–72) the foreign political activity of Kievan Rus reached its zenith. Svyatoslav's armies scored the following spectacular victories:

> c. 965—Sarkel, the Khazar stronghold on the lower Don, was captured and renamed Belaya Vezha.
>
> c. 966—Bulgar, the capital of the Volga Bulgars, was sacked, and their state was subordinated to Russia.
>
> c. 967—the Khazar capital, Itil, was looted. By destroying the great Khazar kaganate, Svyatoslav inadvertently exposed Russia's southeastern frontiers to increasingly serious incursions by the steppe nomads of the east.
>
> c. 967—the major portion of Danubian Bulgaria was occupied, and Svyatoslav established his headquarters at Pereyaslavets, commanding the river delta.

At this point Svyatoslav's vast empire stretched from the mouth of the Volga through the Crimea to the mouth of the Danube. His triumphs were fleeting, however, as he had overextended his forces: he soon had to face widespread revolts in the east and a Byzantine challenge in the west. His capture of the Bulgarian capital, Preslav, in 971 was followed by military reverses that same year: he was defeated by the Byzantine army and forced to abandon his claims to Bulgaria and the Crimea. While withdrawing from the Danube, his army was ambushed by the Pechenegs near the Dnieper cataracts, and Svyatoslav was killed in the ensuing battle (972).

Although most of Svyatoslav's new empire was lost, the territories retained by Russia in 972 (Map 2) constituted a considerable net gain over the area bequeathed by Oleg sixty years earlier.

4

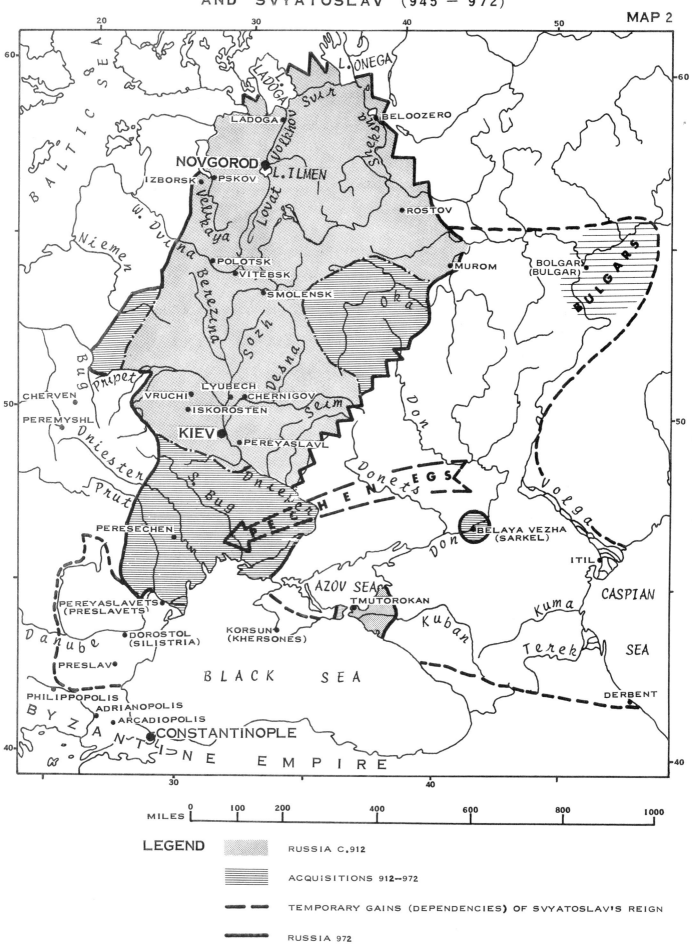

RUSSIA IN THE TIME OF IGOR (C. 912 — 945)
AND SVYATOSLAV (945 — 972)

MAP 2

BALTIC SEA

L. ONEGA

L. LADOGA

LADOGA

BELOOZERO

Volkhov

Sukhona

Sheksna

IZBORSK   PSKOV

NOVGOROD   L. ILMEN

Lovat

Velikaya

ROSTOV

Niemen

W. Dvina

Berezina

POLOTSK

VITEBSK

MUROM

BOLGARY
(BULGAR)

SMOLENSK

Oka

BULGARS

Bug

Pripet

Sozh

Desna

VRUCHI   LYUBECH   CHERNIGOV

CHERVEN

ISKOROSTEN   Seim

PEREMYSHL

KIEV

PEREYASLAVL

Don

Dniester

Dnieper

Donets   EGS

Prut

S. Bug

PETCHENEGS

Volga

PERESECHEN

Don   BELAYA VEZHA
(SARKEL)

ITIL

CASPIAN

PEREYASLAVETS
(PRESLAVETS)

AZOV SEA

TMUTOROKAN

Kuma

SEA

Danube

DOROSTOL
(SILISTRIA)

KORSUN
(KHERSONES)

Kuban

Terek

PRESLAV

BLACK   SEA

DERBENT

PHILIPPOPOLIS

ADRIANOPOLIS

ARCADIOPOLIS

CONSTANTINOPLE

B Y Z A N T I N E   E M P I R E

MILES

0   100   200   400   600   800   1000

LEGEND   RUSSIA C. 912

ACQUISITIONS 912—972

TEMPORARY GAINS (DEPENDENCIES) OF SVYATOSLAV'S REIGN

RUSSIA 972

Map 3. Russia from the Death of Svyatoslav (972) to the Death of Yaroslav (1054)

Kievan Rus at Its Zenith

At the end of a brief period of fraternal conflict over the succession to Svyatoslav's throne, his son Vladimir ("the Saint") emerged as the ruler of Kiev (c. 980–1015). Remembered mainly for converting Russia to Christianity (c. 989), Vladimir also expanded her frontiers to the west. About 981 he seized Peremyshl, Cherven, and the surrounding areas from the Poles. Two years later he conquered the Yatvyags and annexed the area between the middle Niemen and Western Bug rivers (c. 983); further progress toward the Baltic Sea was blocked by Poland. He successfully repulsed several raids by the Pechenegs, building a series of fortifications to bolster the defense of the southern frontier.

Vladimir's death (1015) was followed by renewed and prolonged fratricidal strife, culminating in the division of the realm (1024) between his surviving sons, Mstislav and Yaroslav. The former ruled the area east of the Dnieper River from Chernigov (originally from Tmutorokan), in cooperation with Yaroslav, who ruled the western half of the realm from Novgorod. Upon the death of Mstislav in 1036, Yaroslav reunited the realm and restored Kiev as the capital.

The reign of Yaroslav "the Wise" (1036–54) may be considered the zenith of Kievan Russia's cultural and political development as well as the height of her international prestige. Yaroslav resumed the advance in the west at the expense of the Poles, Lithuanians, and Finns. In 1030 he founded the town of Yurev in the northwest, and subsequent gains in that region secured Novgorod's control of the southeastern littoral of the Gulf of Finland (Ingria). At the time of his death, Kievan Rus was the largest state in Europe, uniting all of the eastern Slavs and including several non-Slavic tribes.

RUSSIA FROM THE DEATH OF SVYATOSLAV (972)
TO THE DEATH OF YAROSLAV (1054)

MAP 3

BALTIC SEA

GULF OF FINLAND

L. ONEGA

L. LADOGA

INGRI

LADOGA

BELOOZERO

YUREV

NOVGOROD

IZBORSK

PSKOV

YAROSLAVL

Niemen

ROSTOV

Volga

TOROPETS

SUZDAL

Dvina

USVYAT

POLOTSK

VITEBSK

MUROM

Kama

SMOLENSK

BULGAR

IZYASLAVL

Oka

Bug

BERESTE

TUROV

RYAZAN

LYUBECH

VRUCHI

CHERNIGOV

KURSK

CHERVEN

VLADIMIR

BELZ

PEREMYSHL

KIEV

VASILEV

PEREYASLAVL

RODNYA

Don

Dniester

S. Bug

Dnieper

Donets

Volga

Prut

BELAYA VEZHA

PERESECHEN

Danube

AZOV SEA

CASPIAN

TMUTOROKAN

Kuban

SEA

Terek

BLACK   SEA

CONSTANTINOPLE

BYZANTINE   EMPIRE

MILES   0   100   200   400   600   800   1000

LEGEND

RUSSIA 972

ACQUISITIONS 972–1054

RUSSIA 1054

Map 4. Russia from 1054 to 1237

The Decline of Kiev

Shortly before his death in 1054, Yaroslav divided the realm among his five sons, setting a precedent that contributed to the intense dynastic strife of succeeding generations. From the middle of the eleventh century until the Mongol conquest in the thirteenth century, the history of Kievan Rus was marked by increasing political disintegration, with the exception of the constructive but brief reign of Vladimir II (1113–25). The nominal primacy of Kiev was contested (except in religious matters) by Novgorod in the northwest, Vladimir in the northeast, and Galicia in the southwest. In 1169 the city was even burned by a Russian army from the rival principality of Vladimir-Suzdal (also known as Rostov-Suzdal and later simply as Vladimir). By the thirteenth century it was no longer possible to rally the land for a united stand to meet the great Mongol challenge.

Economic dislocations and border raiders also contributed to the decline of Kievan Rus. The sacking of Constantinople by the Crusaders in 1204 was one of several factors which adversely affected Kiev's foreign trade. The Polovtsi (or Cumans), who succeeded the Pechenegs as the major threat in the south in the century preceding the Mongol onslaught, devastated the steppes and forced the disunited Russians to withdraw from the mouths of the Dnieper and Southern Bug rivers. This further hampered Kiev's commerce.

In the northwest, powerful new enemies appeared early in the thirteenth century: two Germanic military-religious orders, the Sword Bearers and the Teutonic Order, which united in 1237. The Sword Bearers seized Yurev (renamed Dorpat in 1224 by its new rulers) and threatened both Pskov and Polotsk. They also spread eastward along the right bank of the Western Dvina, seizing the principalities of Kukenois (1208) and Gertsike (1209).

The first modest Lithuanian advances against the principality of Polotsk also began about the turn of the century.

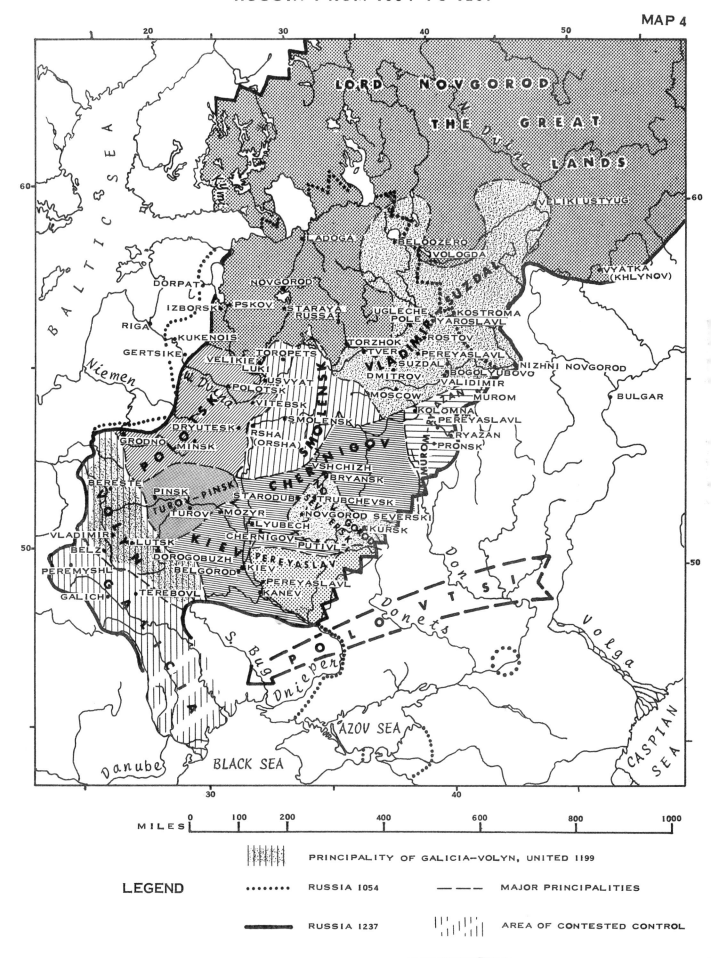

LORD   NOVGOROD

THE   GREAT

LANDS

VELIKI USTYUG

VYATKA
(KHLYNOV)

LADOGA

BELOOZERO

VOLOGDA

BALTIC SEA

DORPAT

NOVGOROD

IZBORSK

PSKOV

STARAYA
RUSSA

UGLECHE
POLE

KOSTROMA

SUZDAL

YAROSLAVL

RIGA

KUKENOIS

TOROPETS

VELIKIE
LUKI

TORZHOK

TVER

ROSTOV

PEREYASLAVL

GERTSIKE

Niemen

USVVAT

POLOTSK

VITEBSK

VLADIMIR

SUZDAL

DMITROV

BOGO-LYUBOVO

VALIDIMIR

NIZHNI NOVGOROD

BULGAR

DRYUTESK

SMOLENSK

MOSCOW

MUROM

GRODNO

RSHA
(ORSHA)

POLOTSK

MINSK

SMOLENSK

CHERNIGOV

VSHCHIZH

KOLOMNA

PEREYASLAVL

RYAZAN

PRONSK

MUROM

BRYANSK

BERESTE

PINSK

TUROV-PINSK

STARODUB

TRUBCHEVSK

TUROV

MOZYR

NOVGOROD SEVERSKI

SIVERSK

KURSK

VOLYN

KIEV

LYUBECH

CHERNIGOV

PUTIVL

VLADIMIR

LUTSK

DOROGOBUZH

BELGOROD

KIEV

PEREYASLAV

BELZ

PEREMYSHL

TEREBOVL

KANEV

PEREYASLAVL

GALICH

GALICIA

POLOVTSI

S. Bug

Dnieper

Donets

Don

Volga

AZOV SEA

CASPIAN SEA

Danube

BLACK SEA

MILES   0   100   200   400   600   800   1000

Although the realm as a whole lost its cohesiveness during this period, certain individual principalities scored notable gains. "Lord Novgorod the Great" expanded her strong economic and weaker political control over vast stretches of the north, from present-day Finland to the Urals and from Lake Ladoga to the White Sea. Sizable gains were also recorded in the northeast by the principality of Vladimir-Suzdal.

The Russian landscape was gradually altered by the founding of scores of new towns and cities during this period. Those shown on Map 4 are only the more important ones; by 1237 nearly 300 towns were scattered throughout the land. The urban concentrations in the northeast and southwest are indicative of the population shifts away from the turbulent southeastern frontier.

Map 5. Russia and the Mongol Conquest

Russia Under Mongol Rule

In 1223 a strong cavalry detachment of Chingis-Khan's Mongols (Tatars, or Tartars) swept out of the Caucasus, defeated both the Polovtsi and the Russians at the Kalka River, raided the Crimean and lower Dnieper areas, wheeled northeast to the middle Volga, where they suffered one of their few reverses (at the hands of the Bulgars), and then disappeared into the vastness of Asia. Since this visitation was only an armed reconnaissance, incidental to the conquest of Khorezm, the Russians saw no more of the mysterious strangers until they returned in force in 1237, this time determined to subjugate the Russians and their neighbors to the west.

The Russian princes did not make a united stand, and the Mongol conquest was thorough and devastating (the course of their campaign is outlined on Map 5). By 1240, when Kiev fell, Russian resistance had virtually ceased. In 1242, upon hearing of the death (in December 1241) of the Great Khan in distant Mongolia, the Mongol vanguard forces withdrew from southeastern Europe, where they had already reached the Adriatic, thereby terminating the westward phase of their great drive for world domination. However, they halted in the lower Volga region, founding the city of Saray above the river delta. This served as the first capital of the khanate of Kypchak, subsequently known as the Golden Horde, which ruled the Russian lands for over two centuries. Another city named Saray was later founded upstream, where the Volga nears the Don; in the fourteenth century the capital was transferred to this "new" Saray.

The successive khans of the Golden Horde summoned the Russian princes to Saray to pay them homage and tribute: even Novgorod, which had not suffered direct attack during the initial conquest, submitted to the humiliation of this Mongol yoke. Only two Russian principalities escaped: Polotsk was never subjugated, and Turov-Pinsk, while partially

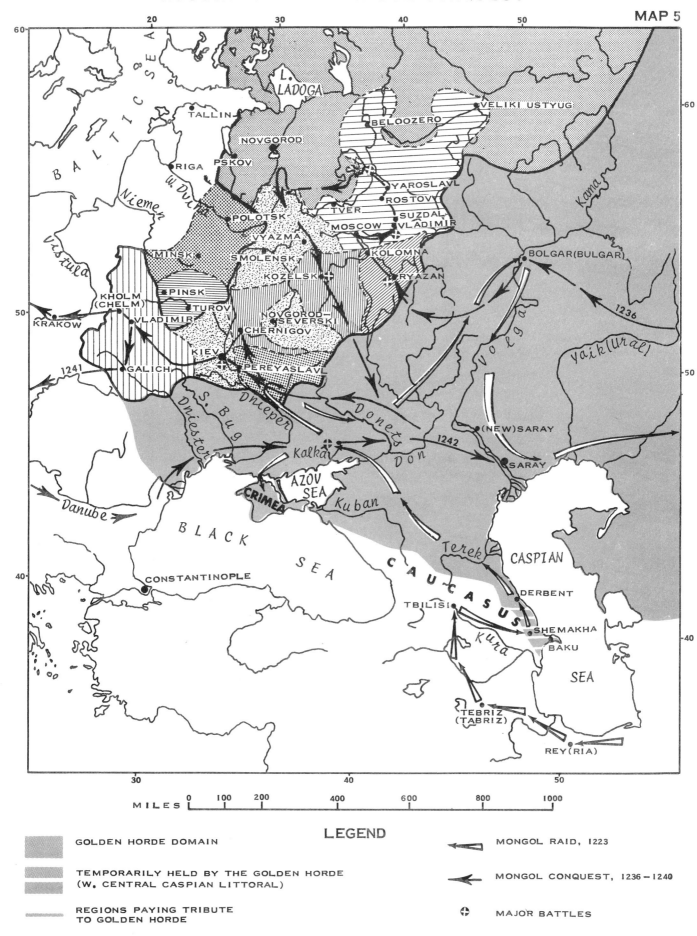

RUSSIA AND THE MONGOL CONQUEST

MAP 5

MILES

0 100 200 400 600 800 1000

LEGEND

GOLDEN HORDE DOMAIN

TEMPORARILY HELD BY THE GOLDEN HORDE
(W. CENTRAL CASPIAN LITTORAL)

REGIONS PAYING TRIBUTE
TO GOLDEN HORDE

MONGOL RAID, 1223

MONGOL CONQUEST, 1236–1240

⊕ MAJOR BATTLES

——— MAJOR RUSSIAN PRINCIPALITIES ABOUT THE TIME OF THE MONGOL CONQUEST sacked by the Mongols, did not pay them tribute. However, within a century both lands were absorbed by Lithuania (see below, page 16).

In a formal, legalistic sense, there was no Russian state during the period of Mongol rule, but only separate Russian principalities, each of whose princes ruled only by virtue of securing a *yarlyk* (patent) from the Khan. Nevertheless, as long as submission, tribute, and conscripts were obtained, the Mongols generally were content to allow considerable local autonomy to their Russian vassals.

Because of this tolerance, "Russia" did not lose territory in the east to the Mongols. However, other incursions during this period resulted in the loss of extensive areas in the west and northwest (for details, see pages 16–18). The Mongols did assume direct control over the southwestern areas, including the Black Sea littoral between the Dniester and Danube rivers; this region had been nominally under the control of Galician princes, but for decades had been contested, and at times dominated, by the Polovtsi.

The decline of Mongol power resulted less from Russian initiative than from internal weaknesses of the pan-Mongol empire, which terminated about 1368, and of the Golden Horde. The latter began to disintegrate in the fifteenth century, when various independent Tartar khanates were established (see Map 10). Finally, in 1480, the pretense of Russian fealty to the Khan was dropped, and shortly afterward (1502) the remnants of the once mighty Horde were annihilated by the rival Crimean Tartars.

The demise of the Golden Horde did not immediately result in the restoration of the Russian state as it had existed in pre-Mongol times. However, in their exercise of local autonomy, the princes (or grand dukes) of Muscovy had begun to consolidate their power during the height of Mongol domination. When the grip of the Horde was finally broken, Muscovy was better prepared than any of the rival principalities to bid for supremacy in creating a unified Russian state.

Map 6. Russian Losses in the West, c. 1237–1462

Western Encroachment During the Mongol Era

While a divided Russia was preoccupied with her Mongol conquerors, neighbors exerted steady pressure on her western frontiers (see Map 6). The initial advances of the Teutonic Knights at the beginning of the thirteenth century were reinforced during its second half; the Knights pushed farther east along the Western Dvina, seizing the northwestern part of the principality of Polotsk.

A more ominous advance began just south of that area, where the newly unified Grand Duchy of Lithuania, led by the Grand Duke Mindovg, began its serious expansion about the middle of the thirteenth century. By the time of Mindovg's death in 1263, Grodno (Gorodna), Novogrudok (Novgorodok), and Slonim had been added to the Lithuanian lands. Mindovg's influence was felt even farther, as the princes of Polotsk and Vitebsk were his relatives.

The princes of western Russia, living under the constant threat of attack by the Teutonic Knights and of punitive Mongol expeditions, often welcomed these Lithuanian advances: the princes of Pinsk, for example, willingly recognized Mindovg as their suzerain. In spite of occasional temporary reverses, the Lithuanians, who had in 1385–86 united by personal union with the Poles, continued to penetrate deep into Russian territory.

Viten, Grand Duke of Lithuania from 1293 to 1316, finally completed the annexation of Polotsk in 1307. Polotsk had enjoyed a unique history; it had been virtually autonomous for a century during the Kievan era (from c. 1024 to c. 1130); and, along with the principality of Turov to its south, shared the proud distinction of never having paid tribute to the Mongols.

Viten's successor, Gedimin (1316–41), expanded his entire southern and eastern boundaries. He secured such important areas as Vitebsk (1318–20), Bereste (Brest, c. 1319), the principality of Turov-Pinsk, and the entire Berezina River basin.

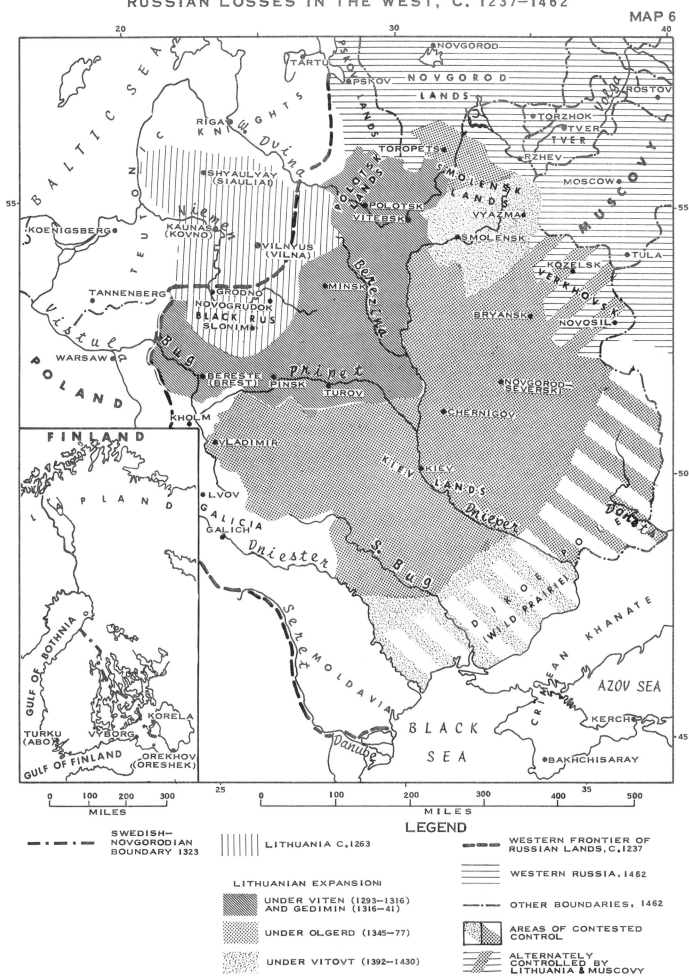

RUSSIAN LOSSES IN THE WEST, C. 1237–1462

MAP 6

BALTIC SEA

TARTU
PSKOV
NOVGOROD
NOVGOROD LANDS
ROSTOV
RIGA
TORZHOK
TVER
TVER
RZHEV
SHYAULYAY (SIAULIAI)
TOROPETS
SMOLENSK LANDS
MOSCOW
MUSCOVY
KOENIGSBERG
KAUNAS (KOVNO)
POLOTSK
VITEBSK
VYAZMA
SMOLENSK
VILNYUS (VILNA)
Berezina
TULA
KOZELSK
VERKHOVSK
TANNENBERG
GRODNO
MINSK
BRYANSK
NOVOSIL
NOVOGRUDOK
BLACK RUS
SLONIM
Vistula
WARSAW
Bug
BERESTE (BREST)
PINSK
TUROV
Pripet
CHERNIGOV
NOVGOROD-SEVERSKI
POLAND
KHOLM
VLADIMIR
KIEV LANDS
KIEV
Dnieper
Donets
LVOV
GALICIA
GALICH
Dniester
S. Bug
D I K O E (WILD PRAIRIE)
Seret
MOLDAVIA
CRIMEAN KHANATE
AZOV SEA
Danube
BLACK SEA
KERCH
BAKHCHISARAY

FINLAND

GULF OF BOTHNIA
L A P L A N D
F I N L A N D
KORELA
TURKU (ABO)
VYBORG
GULF OF FINLAND
OREKHOV (ORESHEK)

0 100 200 300
MILES

0 100 200 300 400 500
MILES

LEGEND

- - · - · - SWEDISH–NOVGORODIAN BOUNDARY 1323

|||| LITHUANIA C. 1263

LITHUANIAN EXPANSION:

UNDER VITEN (1293–1316) AND GEDIMIN (1316–41)

UNDER OLGERD (1345–77)

UNDER VITOVT (1392–1430)

- - - WESTERN FRONTIER OF RUSSIAN LANDS, C. 1237

═══ WESTERN RUSSIA, 1462

- · - · - OTHER BOUNDARIES, 1462

AREAS OF CONTESTED CONTROL

ALTERNATELY CONTROLLED BY LITHUANIA & MUSCOVY

The greatest Lithuanian expansion occurred during the reign of Olgerd (1345–77), which partially coincided with a period of strife within the Golden Horde (c. 1359–81)—an opportunity readily exploited by the Grand Duke. In 1363 Olgerd defeated the Mongols and seized the Black Sea steppes between the mouths of the Southern Bug and the Dniester. Somewhat earlier (1349), the Poles, led by King Casimir, had taken Galicia from the Mongols. While Olgerd's Lithuanian successors retained only tenuous control over the Black Sea littoral, the Poles maintained a firm grip on Galicia. Olgerd held Kiev and the entire Ukraine, except Galicia, and in the northeast he seized Toropets and reached the upper Volga at Rzhev (1355). His successors lost the latter region, but retained the Toropets area, which flanks Smolensk on the north.

The final significant Lithuanian advances into Russian territory occurred during the reign of Vitovt (1392–1430). In addition to pushing the southern frontiers closer to the Black Sea, Vitovt seized the principality of Smolensk in 1395—it was under firm control from 1404—and threatened both Pskov and Novgorod. The principality of Verkhovsk, southeast of Smolensk, was alternately held by Muscovy and Lithuania.

Novgorod was also threatened by Sweden during this period and lost ground in Finland. Novgorod's trade dependencies had extended along the coast of the Gulf of Finland to the Kymi (Kymmene) River and had included most of the sparsely inhabited interior of Finland (see Map 4), but by the close of the thirteenth century Sweden had established the strong fortress of Vyborg (Viipuri) in the heart of Karelia. Although both sides launched attacks along the coast, the situation was essentially a stalemate. This was confirmed, after thirty more years of inconclusive skirmishing, by the Peace of Pahkinasaari (Orekhov, later Schlusselburg) in 1323, establishing the division of southern Finland between Sweden and Novgorod (and later Russia), which endured until 1595 (see insert, Map 6). The boundary with Sweden in the region of the upper Gulf of Bothnia was not mentioned in the 1323 treaty, and the northernmost limits of Novgorod's interests in the west remained undefined. Tribal wars were frequent in the wilds of Lapland, where Swedish-Finnish, Norwegian, and Karelo-Novgorodian interests clashed. The Swedes gradually pushed eastward, gaining de facto control of most of Finland long before the boundary was formally changed at the end of the sixteenth century.

Map 7. The Growth of Muscovy, 1300–1340

Beginnings of Russian Consolidation During the Mongol Era

The next six maps (Nos. 7–12) depict the growth of Muscovy between 1300 and 1533. They do not deal with the expansion of Russia per se, since nearly all of the territory under Muscovite control in 1533 had been part of Kievan Rus prior to the Mongol conquest. Rather, they illustrate the consolidation of power in one of the numerous principalities which were still nominally under Mongol suzerainty until 1480. Muscovy's dramatic growth during this period, at the expense of neighboring Russian principalities, prepared the way for her successful bid for national leadership subsequent to the decline of the Golden Horde.

Moscow, when first mentioned in the Chronicles for 1147 A.D., was only an insignificant town in the large principality of Vladimir. Its growth as a political center, both within the principality and in relation to neighboring areas, was the result of various factors. Geography favored the town, which was surrounded by deep protective forests and located at the strategic center of the river system of European Russia (see Map 7). (In modern times, canals have replaced the earlier portages. With the opening of the Volga-Don Ship Canal in 1952, the Soviets boast that Moscow is a port of five seas, linked, via the Moskva-Volga Canal and others, with the Baltic, White, Black, Azov, and Caspian seas.) The longevity and financial abilities of her princes were contributory factors in Moscow's development; their astute use of the tax power, as agents of the Mongol khans, is a case in point. The prestigious support of the Orthodox Church was also significant; although the see was officially transferred from Kiev to the city of Vladimir in 1300, Metropolitan Peter (installed 1310) preferred to reside in Moscow, and his successor transferred the see there. An important event occurred about 1332, when the Khan elevated the reigning Prince of Moscow, Ivan I, to the position of Grand Duke of Vladimir; thereafter, the two offices remained united. Ivan I willfully embellished his title of Grand Duke of Vladimir and Moscow with the portentous phrase "and of all Russia."

20

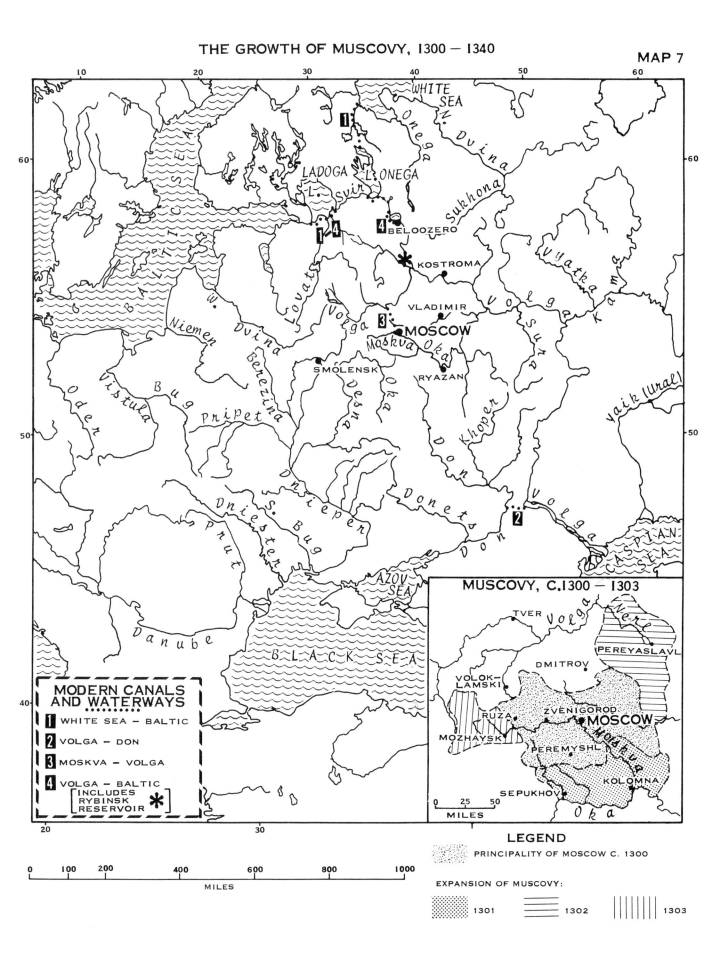

THE GROWTH OF MUSCOVY, 1300 — 1340

MAP 7

WHITE SEA

LADOGA
L. ONEGA
L.
BELOOZERO
KOSTROMA
VLADIMIR
MOSCOW
SMOLENSK
RYAZAN

BALTIC SEA

Oder
Vistula
Niemen
W. Dvina
Bug
Pripet
Berezina
Lovat
Volga
Moskva
Oka
Desna
Don
Khoper
Dnieper
Prut
Dniester
S. Bug
Donets
Don
Volga
Sura
Vyatka
Kama
Yaik (Ural)
CASPIAN SEA

Danube
BLACK SEA
AZOV SEA

N. Dvina
Onega
Sukhona
Svir

MODERN CANALS AND WATERWAYS

1 WHITE SEA – BALTIC
2 VOLGA – DON
3 MOSKVA – VOLGA
4 VOLGA – BALTIC

[INCLUDES RYBINSK RESERVOIR *]

MUSCOVY, C.1300 – 1303

TVER
Volga
Nerl
PEREYASLAVL
DMITROV
VOLOK-LAMSKI
RUZA
ZVENIGOROD
MOSCOW
MOZHAYSK
Moskva
PEREMYSHL
SEPUKHOV
KOLOMNA
Oka

0 25 50
MILES

LEGEND

PRINCIPALITY OF MOSCOW C. 1300

EXPANSION OF MUSCOVY:

1301   1302   1303

0 100 200 400 600 800 1000
MILES

The Muscovite accretions during the first years of the fourteenth century were modest but important. In 1301 Prince Daniel seized the town of Kolomna, at the confluence of the Oka and Moskva rivers, and surrounding areas on the northern bank of the upper Oka. This led to warfare with the Prince of Ryazan, who had possessed Kolomna, and his supporting Mongol troops, but Daniel was victorious and retained the Kolomna region. Shortly afterward (c. 1302) Daniel took advantage of the death of the heirless prince of neighboring Pereyaslavl to occupy that principality northeast of Moscow (it is sometimes designated Pereyaslavl-Zalesski to distinguish it from the other principality of Pereyaslavl, located north of the Dnieper River above its bend, and from Pereyaslavl-Ryazanski on the Oka River). Although this seizure was contested by the reigning Grand Duke of Vladimir, the Khan eventually confirmed Muscovite control. Finally, around 1303, Daniel occupied Mozhaysk, which had belonged to the principality of Smolensk.

As noted above, Ivan I (1325–c. 1341), through skillful diplomacy in his relations with the Mongols, greatly strengthened the position of Muscovy. Although he did not formally annex any new territory, his political influence was widely felt—in Vladimir, for example, and as far north as Beloozero and Kostroma.

Map 8. Muscovy, 1340–1389

The Reigns of Simeon the Proud (c. 1341–1353),
Ivan II (1353–1359), and Dmitri Donskoi (1359–1389)

The reigns of Ivan's sons, Simeon and Ivan II, were marked by protracted troubles with rival Russian principalities, as well as with Lithuania, which gravely threatened the position of Muscovy. Nevertheless, small gains were recorded: in 1341 Simeon acquired the town and region of Yurev (northeast of Moscow—not the Baltic town which had formerly been known by that name). During the reign of Ivan II (1353–59), a larger area southwest of Moscow, which included Borovsk and Vereya, was annexed de facto (although de jure annexation did not follow for another century).

Although the diplomatic situation was even more complex during the following reign, when in addition to Muscovite wars with Lithuania rival khans supported contending Russian princes, Dmitri's gains were the most impressive in Muscovy's history to that time. This dramatic expansion coincided with the beginnings of serious troubles within the Golden Horde—a favorable turn of events which provided the opportunity for Dmitri to achieve the only major Russian victory over the Mongols—in 1380, at Kulikovo Pole near the Don River. (Subsequently Dmitri was heralded by the surname "Donskoi.") Although a new Mongol triumph two years later nullified the practical effects of Dmitri's victory, his success at Kulikovo Pole greatly enhanced the prestige of Muscovy.

About 1364 Dmitri acquired the principalities of Vladimir, Uglich, Kostroma, and Galich (northeast of Moscow—not the Galich, or Galicia, of the Dniester area), as well as the lesser territories surrounding the towns of Dmitrov, Ryapolovo, and Starodub (on the Klyazma River—not the town of this name west of the Desna River). In 1371 he annexed the area around Medyn (south of Borovsk). Between 1362 and the end of his reign in 1389, the Kaluga-Obolensk region to the south of Muscovy

MUSCOVY, 1340 — 1389

MAP 8

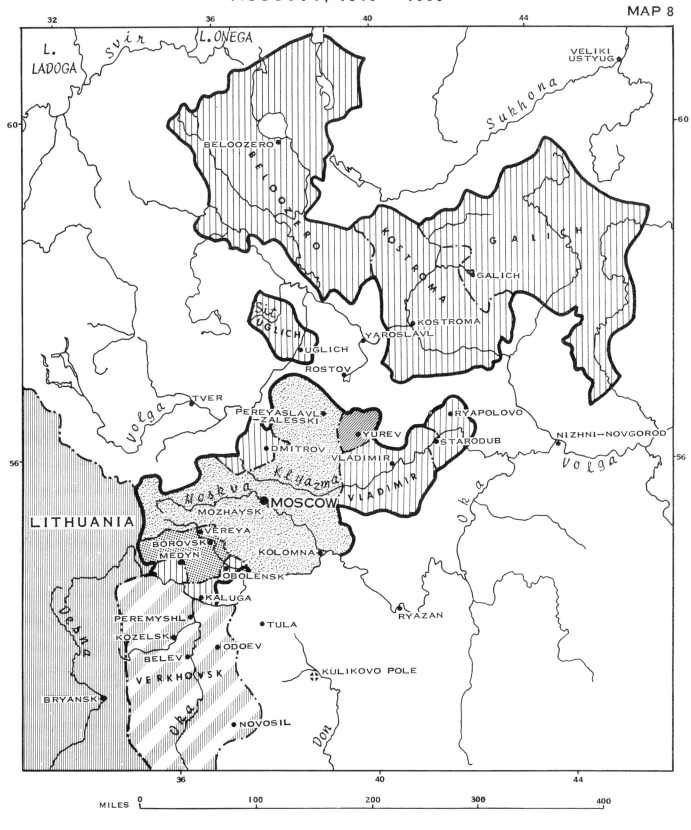

L. LADOGA

L. ONEGA

Svir

Sukhona

VELIKI USTYUG

BELOOZERO

B E L O O Z E R O

KOSTROMA

G A L I C H

GALICH

KOSTROMA

YAROSLAVL

Sit

UGLICH

UGLICH

ROSTOV

TVER

Volga

PEREYASLAVL-ZALESSKI

RYAPOLOVO

YUREV

STARODUB

VLADIMIR

NIZHNI—NOVGOROD

DMITROV

Volga

Klyazma

MOSCOW

Moskva

V L A D I M I R

Oka

LITHUANIA

MOZHAYSK

VEREYA

BOROVSK

MEDYN

KOLOMNA

OBOLENSK

KALUGA

RYAZAN

Desna

PEREMYSHL

TULA

KOZELSK

ODOEV

BELEV

V E R K H O V S K

KULIKOVO POLE

Oka

BRYANSK

NOVOSIL

Don

MILES

0   100   200   300   400

LEGEND

MUSCOVY C. 1340

ANNEXED BY SIMEON (C. 1341–53)

ANNEXED BY IVAN II (1353–59)

ACQUIRED BY DMITRI DONSKOI (1359–89)

ALTERNATELY CONTROLLED BY LITHUANIA AND MUSCOVY

MUSCOVY 1389

and the large Beloozero principality to the north were added (their formal annexation was not consummated until the next century). At various periods, Dmitri also held temporary control over Tver, Ryazan, Starodub, and Trubchevsk (the latter two in the Desna River basin), and even Bulgar, the capital of the Volga Bulgars (see Map 4).

It is worth noting (Map 8) that four of the principalities acquired by Dmitri were not contiguous to the heart of Muscovy. Further "gathering in" of the Russian principalities thus became virtually inevitable.

Map 9. Muscovy, 1389-1425

The Reign of Vasili I (1389-1425)

Dmitri Donskoi's crafty son, Vasili, fluctuated between supporting and opposing the Golden Horde and the Lithuanians, while consistently fighting or outmaneuvering rival Russian princes. About 1393, taking advantage of the contest between Khan Tokhtamysh and his powerful rival, Tamerlane, Vasili secured from the former the patent to the large principality of Nizhni-Novgorod, and also the regions of Gorodets-Meshcherski and Tarusa. The principality of Murom, which lay between the first two areas, was also annexed about this time.

However, it was not until the second decade of the fifteenth century that Vasili succeeded in consolidating his hold over Nizhni-Novgorod (at the junction of the Oka and Volga rivers; not to be confused with "Great" Novgorod in the northwest). He also secured other sizable additions: Rzhev and the headwaters of the Volga, the adjoining area of Khlyapen, and Volokolamsk (all three in the west); Bezhetski Verkh in the northwest; and Vologda and Veliki Ustyug in the northeast.

Vasili also reduced the Mordvinians, who inhabited the exposed salient in the southeast of his realm, to a semi-dependent status. By the end of his reign, all of the Muscovite territories were contiguous; but there still remained some obviously vulnerable independent principalities jutting into the very heart of Muscovy (see Map 9), foretelling even further annexations.

MUSCOVY, 1389 — 1425

MAP 9

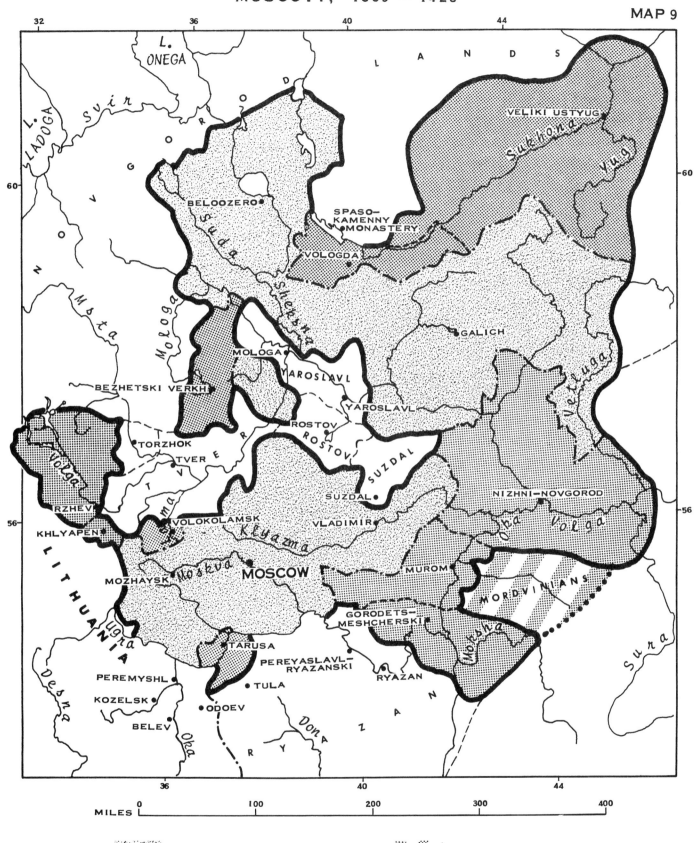

L. ONEGA

L. LADOGA

N O V G O R O D

Svir

Msta

Mologa

Suda

VELIKI USTYUG

Sukhona

Yug

BELOOZERO

SPASO-KAMENNY MONASTERY

VOLOGDA

Shekhsna

GALICH

Vetluga

MOLOGA

YAROSLAVL

BEZHETSKI VERKH

YAROSLAVL

ROSTOV

ROSTOV

SUZDAL

TORZHOK

T V E R

SUZDAL

NIZHNI—NOVGOROD

Volga

TVER

VLADIMIR

RZHEV

VOLOKOLAMSK

Klyazma

Oka

Volga

KHLYAPEN

Moskva

MOSCOW

MUROM

LITHUANIA

MOZHAYSK

MORDVINIANS

Ugra

Mokhsa

GORODETS-MESHCHERSKI

TARUSA

PEREYASLAVL-RYAZANSKI

Sura

Desna

PEREMYSHL

TULA

RYAZAN

KOZELSK

ODOEV

R Y A Z A N

BELEV

Oka

Don

0   100   200   300   400

MILES

LEGEND

MUSCOVY 1389

SEMI—DEPENDENCY OF MUSCOVY

ACQUIRED BY VASILI I

MUSCOVY 1425

Map 10. Muscovy, 1425–1462

The Reign of Vasili II (1425–1462)

The turbulent reign of Vasili II witnessed much strife but only minor territorial gains. Engaged in a prolonged feud with his uncle, Yuri, and the latter's sons, and frequently forced to repel Mongol raids, Vasili was barely able to retain the territory he had inherited. Indeed, he twice lost and twice regained his throne. Nevertheless, in 1451 he annexed what remained of the ancient principality of Suzdal, and by the end of the reign he had also acquired Tula in the south and the area surrounding the Spaso-Kamenny Monastery in the north. In addition, he secured tenuous control over Ryazan in 1447 and over Novgorod in 1456.

Although Muscovy was repeatedly engaged in inconclusive skirmishes with Mongol detachments during Vasili's reign, the Golden Horde itself was visibly disintegrating at that time. In the second quarter of the century the Crimean Tartars established their independent khanate around the Sea of Azov (it became an Ottoman vassalage in 1475); the khanate of Kazan was established in the Kama-Volga river area around 1445; and the Astrakhan khanate in the lower Volga basin about 1460 (see Map 10).

The enlistment of numerous Tartar princes in the service of Vasili was symbolic both of the declining power of the Golden Horde and of the maturing status of Muscovy. About 1453 the "Kingdom" of Kasimov was established on Russia's southeastern frontier, centered on the old town of Gorodets-Meshcherski on the Oka River. This vassal Tartar state served as a defensive buffer for Moscow against the incursions of hostile Mongol forces. While still nominally subject to the khan at Saray, by the end of his reign Vasili was virtually independent; the balance of power had shifted decisively in favor of Muscovy.

MUSCOVY, 1425 – 1462

MAP 10

20 · 40 · 60

S W E D E N

BALTIC SEA

WHITE SEA

N. Dvina

L. ONEGA

VYBORG

L. LADOGA

60

LIVONIA

VELIKI USTYUG

BELOOZERO

SPASO-KAMENNY MONASTERY

PSKOV · NOVGOROD

VOLOGDA

RIGA

GALICH

W. Dvina

YAROSLAVL

Kama

VILNA

ROSTOV · TVER

SUZDAL

KAZAN

POLOTSK · RZHEV

KAZAN KHANATE

SMOLENSK

MOSCOW

MINSK

GORODETS-MESHCHERSKI (KASIMOV)

KOZELSK

PEREYASLAVL-RYAZANSKI

BELEV

TULA

RYAZAN

L I T H U A N I A

STARODUB · ODOEV

Oka

PINSK

NOVOSIL

CHERNIGOV

ELETS

50

KIEV

Yaik (Ural)

CHERKASSY

Volga

Dniester

Don

SARAY

MOLDAVIA

Dnieper

ASTRAKHAN KHANATE

KHANATE

C R I M E A N

AZOV

ASTRAKHAN

CASPIAN

KHANATE

KERCH

BAKHCHISARAY

B L A C K   S E A

SEA

30 · 40 · 50

MILES

0   100   200   400   600   800   1000

LEGEND

MUSCOVY 1425

MUSCOVY 1462

GENERAL BORDERS OF RUSSIAN LANDS 1462

ACQUIRED BY VASILI II

OTHER INTERNATIONAL BORDERS 1462

Map 11. Muscovy, 1462–1505

The Reign of Ivan III (1462–1505)

In foreign affairs the reign of Ivan III, or "the Great," is noteworthy on two counts: the end of the Mongol yoke is traditionally (and somewhat arbitrarily) dated 1480, the year when this cautious Grand Duke outsat an even more cautious Mongol Khan at the Ugra River; and the Muscovite territory was expanded more by Ivan than by all his predecessors combined (see Map 11).

In 1463 the principality of Yaroslavl, which had been virtually surrounded by Muscovy, joined Ivan's realm. At the same time, Ivan purchased about half of the adjoining principality of Rostov. Eleven years later, the princes of Rostov—no doubt reading the handwriting on the encircling walls—sold the remainder of their lands and entered the service of Muscovy.

In 1472 Ivan conquered and annexed the Perm lands, along the Kama River. In 1489 he took possession of the Vyatka lands, centered on the town of Khlynov (Vyatka) on the Vyatka River; two years earlier a Muscovite army had captured Kazan, installing a vassal khan on the throne. On several occasions, Ivan's forces campaigned as far as the northern Urals and slightly beyond, annexing an area extending to the lower Ob River. Part of these gains in the northeast were areas which had never been under Russian control, even during the greatest period of Kievan Rus.

Ivan's major triumph came in 1478, with the final conquest of Novgorod. Along with that great commercial city were annexed its vast dependencies, stretching to the Arctic Ocean and to the Gulf of Finland. In the latter area, Ivan built in 1492 a fortified port, Ivangorod, near the mouth of the Narova River and opposite the German town of Narva. Thus, long before Peter I, Russia had a "window to the West."

In 1485 Ivan conquered and annexed Tver, which had been the most important Russian principality still independent after the fall of Nov-

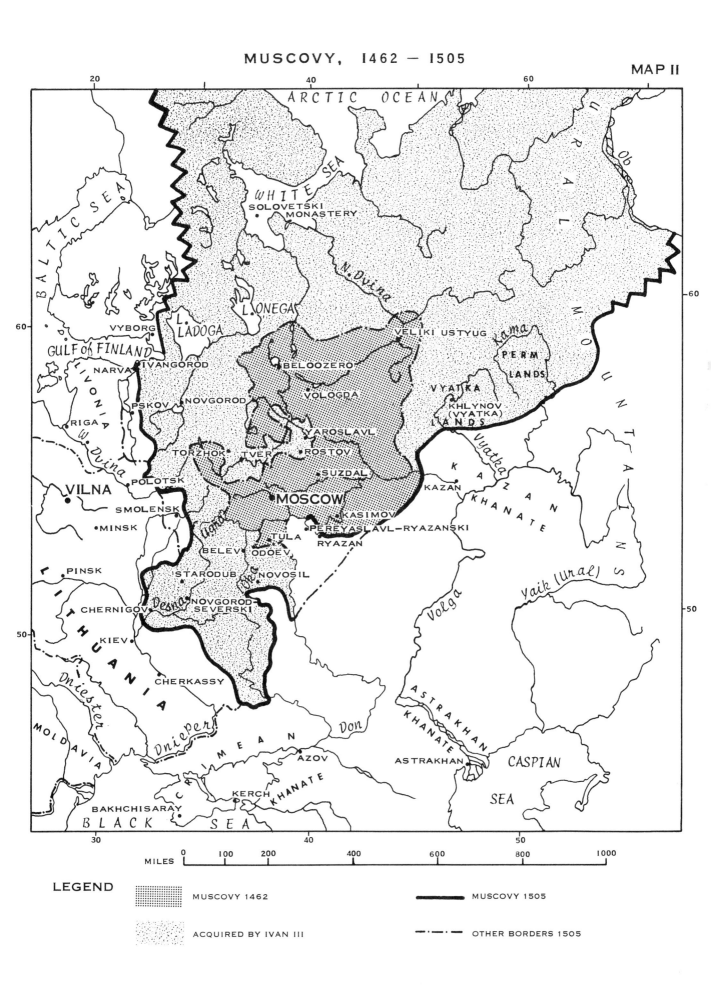

MUSCOVY, 1462 — 1505

MAP II

ARCTIC OCEAN

BALTIC SEA

WHITE SEA

SOLOVETSKI MONASTERY

URAL MOUNTAINS

Ob

N. Dvina

VYBORG

L. ONEGA

L. LADOGA

VELIKI USTYUG

Kama

PERM LANDS

GULF OF FINLAND

IVANGOROD

BELOOZERO

VYATKA

LIVONIA

NARVA

VOLOGDA

KHLYNOV (VYATKA) LANDS

RIGA

PSKOV

NOVGOROD

YAROSLAVL

W. Dvina

TORZHOK

TVER

ROSTOV

Vyatka

POLOTSK

SUZDAL

KAZAN

KAZAN KHANATE

VILNA

MOSCOW

SMOLENSK

KASIMOV

MINSK

Ugra

TULA

PEREYASLAVL—RYAZANSKI

BELEV

ODOEV

RYAZAN

PINSK

STARODUB

NOVOSIL

Oka

Volga

Yaik (Ural)

LITHUANIA

CHERNIGOV

Desna

NOVGOROD-SEVERSKI

Dnieper

KIEV

CHERKASSY

Dniester

Don

ASTRAKHAN KHANATE

MOLDAVIA

C R I M E A N

AZOV

ASTRAKHAN

CASPIAN

KHANATE

KERCH

SEA

BAKHCHISARAY

BLACK   SEA

| 0 | 100 | 200 | 400 | 600 | 800 | 1000 |

MILES

LEGEND

MUSCOVY 1462

MUSCOVY 1505

ACQUIRED BY IVAN III

OTHER BORDERS 1505

gorod; about 1500 the Grand Duke inherited the western half of the principality of Ryazan.

Finally, significant gains were also made in the southwest. Part of these lands (for example, Odoev and Novosil) had long been contested and alternately controlled by Muscovy and Lithuania. Although Lithuania had secured the upper Oka River basin early in the 1400s, by the end of the century Muscovy was in control of the region. During the last decades of Ivan's reign, many of the princes of western Russia voluntarily deserted Lithuania to enter the service of Muscovy. In 1500 the princes of Novgorod-Severski, Chernigov (both on the Desna River), and Starodub (west of that river) entered Ivan's service.

By the end of his reign, only two Great Russian areas were still independent: the eastern half of the principality of Ryazan and the city and region of Pskov. The latter, moreover, was partially under Muscovite control.

Map 12. Muscovy, 1505–1533

The Reign of Vasili III (1505–1533)

The "gathering in" of the Great Russian lands had been virtually completed during Ivan III's reign; his son, Vasili III, merely reinforced the bonds of union. In 1510 Vasili formally annexed Pskov, which had retained a semi-autonomous status after the fall of Novgorod in 1478, and about 1521 he acquired the remaining half of the principality of Ryazan.

Vasili's only striking territorial gain was the capture in 1514 of Smolensk, which had been held by Lithuania since 1404. Although faced with continuing incursions by the Crimean Tartars and revolts in the east by the Kazan khans, Muscovy was at this time strong enough to protect her western acquisitions from Lithuanian attacks.

The consolidation of the Grand Ducal power within Muscovy had proceeded apace with its external growth under Ivan III and Vasili III. While the specific details are beyond the scope of this narrative, it may be noted in passing that the political and psychological foundations had been laid for the establishment of the tsardom of Ivan IV: a consolidated "Muscovy" was ready to become "Russia."

MUSCOVY, 1505 – 1533

MAP 12

BALTIC SEA

WHITE SEA

SOLOVETSKI MONASTERY

Ob

N. Dvina

VYBORG

L. LADOGA

L. ONEGA

VELIKI USTYUG

NARVA · IVANGOROD

BELOOZERO

LIVONIA

PSKOV · NOVGOROD

VOLOGDA

RIGA

W. Dvina

KHLYNOV (VYATKA)

POLOTSK

YAROSLAVL

TVER · ROSTOV

SUZDAL

VILNA

SMOLENSK

MOSCOW

KASIMOV

KAZAN

KAZAN KHANATE

MINSK

PEREYASLAVL – RYAZANSKI

RYAZAN

TULA

PINSK

LITHUANIA

STARODUB

Oka

CHERNIGOV

NOVGOROD SEVERSKI

Volga

Yaik (Ural)

KIEV

CHERKASSY

Dniester

ASTRAKHAN KHANATE

OTTOMAN EMPIRE

Dnieper

CRIMEAN

Don

AZOV

ASTRAKHAN

CASPIAN SEA

KERCH

KHANATE

BAKHCHISARAY

BLACK SEA

MILES

| 0 | 100 | 200 | 400 | 600 | 800 | 1000 |

LEGEND

MUSCOVY 1505

ACQUIRED BY VASILI III

MUSCOVY 1533

OTHER BORDERS 1533

Map 13. Russia, 1533–1598

The Reigns of Ivan IV (1533–1584)
and Fedor (1584–1598)

The foreign adventures of Ivan IV (Grand Duke from 1533; crowned as first "Tsar of All the Russias" in 1547; died 1584) were marked by spectacular successes in the east and dismal failure in the west.

In 1552 Ivan conquered the Tartar khanate of Kazan. Within five years, all of the tribes in that general area (Chuvashi, Mari, Udmurty, and Bashkiry) had joined Russia.

In 1556 Russian forces subjugated the khanate of Astrakhan, bringing the entire Volga River basin under Ivan's control (see Map 13). A year later, the Tsar took under his protection both the Kabarda princes and the Great Nogai Horde (northern Caucasus area and east of the lower Volga respectively). About the same time, the Cherkesy, who inhabited the region south of the Kuban River, became Russian vassals. Subsequently, to protect and exploit these newly acquired regions, numerous fortress towns were established behind the southeastern frontier, including Samara, Voronezh (both in 1586), and Tsaritsyn (1589).

These dramatic eastern advances symbolized the reversal of the Tartar–Moslem tide. In a sense, Ivan became the heir of the Golden Horde, and he ruled a truly multinational "empire," although that term was not formally adopted until 1721. The way was opened for further eastward expansion. This began through private initiative, about 1581, when the Cossack Yermak undertook the conquest of western Siberia; the task was nominally completed about 1584 with the defeat of Khan Kuchum's poorly armed Tartars in the lower Irtysh River basin.

In contrast to his triumphs in the east, Ivan's expansionist efforts in the west were effectively checked. What began in 1558 as simply a Russian invasion of Livonia (then roughly comprising modern Latvia and Estonia) developed into a war with Sweden, Poland, and Lithuania that lasted until 1583. In the meantime, Poland had virtually absorbed Lithuania, after the Lublin Union in 1569. The peace with Poland in

38

RUSSIA. 1533 — 1598

MAP 13

ARCTIC OCEAN

LAPLAND

PECHENGA MONASTERY

KOLA

KEM

WHITE SEA

SOLOVETSKI MONASTERY

NOVO-KHOLMOGORY
(ARKHANGELSK)

KHOLMOGORY

Pechora

OBDORSK

BEREZOV

SURGUT

Ob

NARYM

OBSKI GORODOK

Yenisei

BALTIC SEA

FINLAND

VYBORG

KEXHOLM

L. LADOGA

INGRIA

ORESHEK

IVANGOROD

GDOV

LIVONIA

PSKOV

NOVGOROD

SEBEZH

POLOTSK

TVER

MINSK

SMOLENSK

BELOOZERO

VOLOGDA

ALEKSANDROVA
SLOBODA

VLADIMIR

MOSCOW

KOLOMNA

KALUGA

MUROM

KASIMOV

TULA

W. Dvina

N. Dvina

SOL-VYCHEGODSK

VELIKI USTYUG

Kama

KHLYNOV

KANKOR

VERKHNE-
CHUSOVSKOI

PELYM

VERKHOTURE

TOBOLSK

TYUMEN

KASHLYK
(SIBIR)

TARA

Ob

Tobol

Intysh

NIZHNI-NOVGOROD

KAZAN

KAZAN

SVIYAZHSK

ALATYR KHANATE

UFA

Sura

Oka

OREL

ELETS

VORONEZH

SAMARA

GREAT

Yaik (Ural)

P O L A N D

CHERNIGOV

KIEV

BELGOROD

SARATOV

Volga

Dnieper

SECH
(SICH)

OCHAKOV

PEREKOP

Donets

Don

AZOV

TSARITSYN

ASTRAKHAN
KHANATE

ASTRAKHAN

N O G A I   H O R D E

ARAL
SEA

Syr-Darya

CRIMEAN

BAKHCHISARAY

KHANATE

CHERKESY

Kuban

KABARDA

Terek

CAUCASUS MTS.

BLACK SEA

OTTOMAN
EMPIRE

CASPIAN

SEA

MILES 0 100 200 400 600 800 1000

LEGEND

RUSSIA 1533   ACQUIRED BY IVAN IV & FEDOR   RUSSIA 1598

1582 merely cost Ivan the gains he had won in Livonia during the early years of the war, but the peace with Sweden (1583) cost him all of the Russian possessions on the Gulf of Finland (Ingria), as well as the western shore of Lake Ladoga, including Kexholm, the Swedish name for the early settlement of Korela. Fortunately, the accidental discovery of the route to Russia via the White Sea by English merchant explorers in 1553 partially compensated for the loss of outlets on the Baltic. In 1584 the port Arkhangelsk (called Novo-Kholmogory until 1613) was founded at the mouth of the Northern Dvina River.

The only territorial gain in the west which was retained during Ivan's reign was the capture of the Sebezh area (northwest of Polotsk) from Lithuania in 1535, when Ivan was a child. This area was subsequently seized by Poland early in the seventeenth century.

The fourteen years following Ivan's death, when Boris Gudunov made the decisions for Ivan's feeble-minded son, Fedor, saw a continuation of the same foreign policies. After a new and successful war with Sweden, the Treaty of Tyavzin in 1595 restored Russia's losses of 1583, including Ivangorod and Kexholm. The treaty also established the first complete frontier between Russia and Swedish Finland, from the Arctic Ocean to the Gulf of Finland. This boundary constituted a considerable loss for Russia, in comparison with the 1323 treaty line (see insert, Map 6). In the extreme north, Russia yielded her claim to much of Lapland, a coastal area long disputed by Norwegians, Swedes, and Russians (although the Russians had never occupied the region).

In Siberia, Russia made further gains, after subduing a native revolt that cost Yermak his life (c. 1585). Obski Gorodok, the first Russian settlement in Siberia, was founded in 1585; among other military and fur-trading posts were the future cities of Tyumen (1586), Tobolsk (1587), Surgut (1594), and Narym (c. 1596). By the last date, the greater part of the Ob River basin had been claimed by Russia.

The grandiose external gains of Ivan's reign were offset by internal weaknesses, but their full effect was not evident until the Rurik dynasty died out in 1598.

40

Map 14. Russian Losses, 1598–1618

The Time of the Troubles and Its Aftermath

The chaos, anarchy, and confusion following the extinction of the Rurik dynasty in 1598 provided a tempting opportunity for Russia's western enemies. During the "troubled" years between Fedor's death and the coronation of the first Romanov tsar in 1613, both the Poles and the Swedes seized important western areas, the former even holding Moscow temporarily.

Although all of the complex campaigns of this period need not be traced, the highlights and the legacy should be noted. In 1611 Smolensk fell to the Poles after a twenty-month siege, and that same year Novgorod accepted Swedish suzerainty. By 1613 the Swedes were in control in the northwest, from Lake Ladoga south to Lake Ilmen and west to the Gulf of Finland (see Map 14). By 1612 the Poles had occupied an even larger area, including Moscow itself.

Although the situation was extremely precarious, the Russians rallied and defeated the attempts to impose foreign domination on the country. By the terms of the Peace of Stolbovo in 1617, Sweden withdrew from Novgorod, but retained most of the Lake Ladoga area (including Kexholm), the territory north of that lake, and Ingria. Since the Swedes had acquired Estonia in the sixteenth century, the addition of Ingria gave them control of the entire littoral of the Gulf of Finland. Russia was again cut off from the West via the Baltic Sea.

The Polish threat was more ominous. In 1618 a Polish army advanced on Moscow again, but failed to take the city. By the terms of the Armistice of Deulino (1618), Poland retained the provinces of Smolensk and Seversk (the latter centered at Novgorod-Severski), and a strip of varying width along most of Russia's western border.

None of the parties was prepared to accept these settlements as final; the inconclusive foreign intervention during the "Time of the Troubles" merely set the stage for future wars.

RUSSIAN LOSSES, 1598–1618

MAP 14

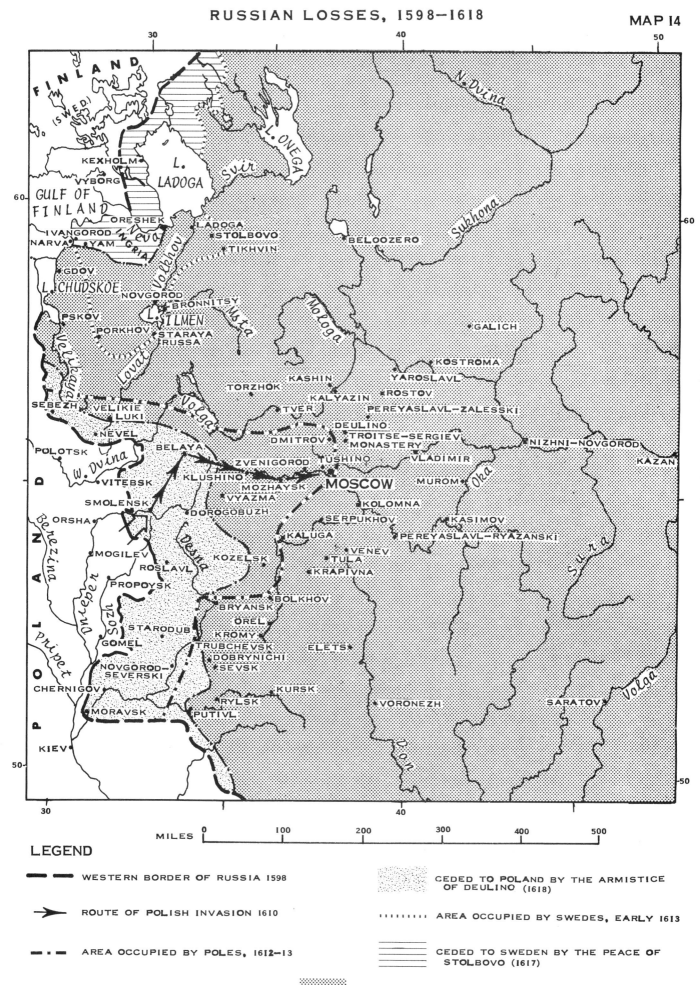

LEGEND

▬ ▬ ▬ WESTERN BORDER OF RUSSIA 1598

━━▶ ROUTE OF POLISH INVASION 1610

▬ · ▬ · ▬ AREA OCCUPIED BY POLES, 1612–13

░░░ CEDED TO POLAND BY THE ARMISTICE OF DEULINO (1618)

········· AREA OCCUPIED BY SWEDES, EARLY 1613

═══ CEDED TO SWEDEN BY THE PEACE OF STOLBOVO (1617)

░░░ EUROPEAN RUSSIA 1618

Map 15. European Russia, 1618–1689

The Ukraine Between Poland and Russia

The Russian state which rallied around the new Romanov dynasty lost little time in seeking revenge for the Polish invasions at the beginning of the century. The attempt to liberate Smolensk in 1632 ended in failure, and the Peace of Polyanovka in 1634 resulted in only minor boundary changes in Russia's favor (see Map 15). However, in 1648 long-smoldering unrest in the Ukraine flared into open warfare between the Zaporozhie Cossacks, led by Bogdan Khmelnitsky, and the Poles. This, in turn, led to a new war between Poland and Russia (1654–67), after Tsar Alexi took the Cossacks under his protection. Poland and the Ukraine suffered considerably in this period, as Swedes, Crimean Tartars, and Cossacks each fought inconclusively on alternating sides, complicating the Russo-Polish conflict and devastating both Poland and the Ukraine in the process.

As a result, a weakened Poland had to make major concessions to Russia by the Armistice of Andrusovo (1667). Russia regained Smolensk, which she had captured early in the war, Chernigov, the entire left bank Ukraine (the Ukraine east of the Dnieper River), and Kiev on the right bank. The latter city and the surrounding area were supposedly transferred for only two years, but the Russians refused to yield their ancient capital when that period expired. By an agreement in 1678, Poland "exchanged" Kiev for a small strip of territory in the northwest which Russia had regained in 1667, including the towns of Sebezh and Nevel. These Russian gains, including the possession of Kiev, were confirmed by the "Eternal Peace" of 1686. Russia's attempts to repossess the western lands of the old state of Kievan Rus had begun in an auspicious fashion.

In 1667 Poland and Russia had agreed to joint "protection" of the Zaporozhie stronghold (the Sech), but in the 1686 settlement the Poles yielded their interest in the area to Russia. Meanwhile dissension among the Cossacks had resulted in their separation into rival groups, divided roughly along the line of the Dnieper River. Turkish influence was strong in the right bank area late in the seventeenth century, and even on the left bank Russian influence remained very tenuous for decades to come.

44

EUROPEAN RUSSIA, 1618–1689

MAP 15

BALTIC SEA

FINLAND

L.
LADOGA

KEXHOLM
VYBORG
ORESHEK
STOLBOVO
TALLIN
NARVA
ESTONIA
YAM
GDOV
LIVONIA
(swed. from 1629)
PSKOV
NOVGOROD
RIGA

W. Dvina

POLA
SEBEZH
NEVELJ
VELIZH
VILNA
VITEBSK
VELIKI LUKI
RZHEV
ANDRUSOVO
SMOLENSK
SERPEYSK
ROSLAVL
BRYANSK
TRUBCHEVSK
CHERNIGOV
GLUKHOV
PUTIVL
NEZHIN
KIEV
BELAYA
TSERKOV
AKHTYRKA

Pripetz

Dniester
Prut
S. Bug
Danube
OTTOMAN EMPIRE

Dnieper

ZAPOROZHIE
KODAK
SECH

CRIMEAN
BAKHCHISARAY
AZOV SEA
K H A N A T E
Kuban
CHERKESY

B L A C K   S E A

ARKHANGELSK

N. Dvina

VELIKI USTYUG

BELOOZERO
VOLOGDA
GALICH
KHLYNOV
KUNGUR

Kama

YAROSLAVL
TVER
TROITSE-SERGIEV
MONASTERY
MOSCOW
VLADIMIR
NIZHNI-NOVGOROD
KAZAN
MENZELINSK
UFA
ARZAMAS
TEMNIKOV
BILYARSK
PEREYASLAVL-RYAZANSKI
TULA
ODOEV
SHATSK
SARANSK
SIMBIRSK
RYAZHSK
VERKHNI
LOMOV
SYZRAN
KOZLOV
PENZA
SAMARA

Ora

TAMBOV
SARATOV
VORONEZH
BELGOROD
OSTROGOZHSK
KHARKOV

Donetz

Yaik (Ural)

Volga

TSARITSYN
Don
CHERKASSK
CHERNY YAR
ASTRAKHAN
KRASNY YAR

C A S P I A N   S E A

AZOV
TERSKI
GORODOK
Terek

LEGEND

EUROPEAN RUSSIA 1618	CEDED TO POLAND IN EXCHANGE FOR KIEV (1678)
CEDED TO RUSSIA BY THE PEACE OF POLYANOVKA (1634)	WESTERN RUSSIAN BOUNDARY 1689
CEDED TO RUSSIA BY THE ARMISTICE OF ANDRUSOVO (1667)	OTHER BOUNDARIES 1689

MILES
0   100   200   400   600   800   1000

Map 16. Eastward Expansion, 1598–1689

The Conquest of Siberia

The pacification of Kuchum's west Siberian khanate in the sixteenth century eliminated the last major organized force between European Russia and the Pacific Ocean. In the seventeenth century, Russian fur traders rolled the frontier steadily eastward, much as French fur traders were penetrating the Canadian wilds about the same time. The Cossacks exacted tribute in furs from the primitive natives and established small garrisons along the river routes through the vast wilderness. Only in the south, where the Russians encountered ancient civilizations, was their advance seriously impeded.

In 1632 the outpost of Yakutsk was established in the middle Lena River valley; around 1649 Okhotsk, on the northern shore of the sea of the same name, was founded. About the same time, the fort of Anadyrski Ostrog (later renamed Markovo) was established in the middle Anadyr River basin.

By 1689 Russia had claimed all of the territory to the Pacific, excluding Kamchatka. However, the small and unruly Cossack garrisons were not always in effective control of this vast area, and native revolts were common, especially in the extreme northeast where the terrain and climate seriously hampered the Russians.

Meanwhile, Russian influence was gradually extended along the southern fringes of the great wilderness. About 1645 Gurev was founded near the mouth of the Yaik (later Ural) River, and the right bank of that river came under Russian control. A few years later (1652), and far to the east, Irkutsk was founded near the southwestern end of Lake Baykal.

The only really effective check to Russia's eastward expansion in the seventeenth century was encountered in the Amur River basin. Russian forces from Yakutsk began the exploration of the Amur region in 1643, alienated the local tribes in the process, and consequently suffered heavy casualties. The most notable of these expeditions were those led by Khabarov from 1649 to 1652; Khabarov's ruthless massacres forced the natives to appeal to the Manchu Emperor for help.

ARCTIC OCEAN

20 40 60 80 100 120 140 160 180

60

ANADYRSKI OSTROG

NIZHNE-KOLYMSK

SREDNE-KOLYMSK

VERKHNE-KOLYMSK

PODSHIVERSK
ZASHIVERSK

VERKHOYANSK

ARKHANGELSK

OBDORSK

BEREZOV

ZHIGANSK

Kolyma

OKHOTSK

MANGAZEYA
TURUKHANSK

Lower Tunguska

VILYUYSK

YAKUTSK

NIZHNI-NOVGOROD

KAZAN

MENZELINSK

VERKHOTURE

SURGUT

Ob

Lena

OLEKMINSK

SEA of OKHOTSK

KAMCHATKA

UFA

TURINSK

TOBOLSK

TYUMEN

ISHIM   TARA

NARYM

YENISEYSK

KIRENSK

VERKHNE-ANGARSK

STANOVOY MTS.

Uda

Amur

YAITSKI GORODOK

Volga

Ural

Ishim   Irtysh

TOMSK

KRASNOYARSK

KUZNETSK

ILIMSK

BRATSKI OSTROG

L. Baykal

ALBAZIN

Argun

Sungari

GUREV

BALAGANSK

IRKUTSK

BARGUZIN

NERCHINSK

AIGUN

Amur

ARAL

SEA

L. Balkhash

VERKHNEUDINSK

A

60

40

40

KHIVA

TASHKENT   KULDZHA

URGA

C   H   I   N   A

LEGEND

RUSSIAN TERRITORY 1598

EXPANSION IN ASIA, 1598–1689

ASIATIC RUSSIA 1689

100
0   200   400   600   800   1000

MILES

60   80   100   120

The Russian fort at Albazin on the upper Amur (first established c. 1650) was the scene of repeated and costly battles for the better part of three decades. Here the Cossacks encountered a more sophisticated enemy than anywhere else in Siberia; although the Chinese still used bows and arrows, they also employed cannon.

After some forty-odd years of inconclusive skirmishing (some encounters occurring as far south as the Sungari River), a negotiated peace was arranged at Nerchinsk in 1689. This treaty, which remained effective for over a century and a half, was a diplomatic victory for China. The boundary (supposedly provisional in the Uda River area) was drawn mainly along the watershed of the Stanovoy Mountains, thus excluding Russians from both banks of the Amur and from all its tributaries east of the Argun River.

Map 17. European Russia, 1689–1725

Peter I and the Russian Empire

The dynamic reign of Peter I ("the Great") witnessed nearly constant warfare, culminating in a stalemate with Turkey and only transitory gains in Persia, but a victory over Sweden that resulted in permanent and strategically significant annexations in the northwest.

In his early campaigns against the Turks and their Crimean Tartar vassals, Peter pushed down the Dnieper and the Don valleys. In the former area, he succeeded in 1695 in establishing several forts, including Kamenny Zaton opposite the Zaporozhie Sech, which greatly increased Russian influence over the Cossacks. In the Don area, he finally captured Azov (1696) and established a new naval base, Taganrog, on the Sea of Azov. These gains were confirmed by the Treaty of Constantinople in 1700.

However, after a large Turkish-Tartar force surrounded Peter's much smaller army at the Prut (Pruth) River in 1711, he was forced to surrender all of these gains. The Peace of Adrianople (1713) confirmed the Prut terms: Russia had to abandon Azov and Taganrog, along with the new fleet based on those ports, and the Dnieper River forts. Turkey also extended her control over the Zaporozhie Cossacks. Nevertheless, from this time onward the Ottoman Empire was permanently on the defensive against Russia.

The results of the Great Northern War with Sweden (1700–21) were more important. By 1703 Peter had conquered Ingria and founded St. Petersburg, which became his new capital a decade later. When the long struggle finally ended with the Treaty of Nystadt (1721), Russia acquired a very large "window" on the Baltic: in addition to Ingria, she annexed Estonia (which Sweden had acquired late in the sixteenth century), Livonia (which the Swedes had wrested from the Poles in the seventeenth century; most of this area had never been held by Russia), and the Dago and Osel islands. Sweden also ceded large areas in southeastern Finland, including Kexholm and Vyborg provinces. The new boundary line along

EUROPEAN RUSSIA, 1689–1725

MAP 17

FINLAND

TAMMERFORS
NYSTADT
ABO
VYBORG
KEXHOLM
L. LADOGA
PETROVSKI
(PETROZAVODSK)

N. Dvina
Kama

VERKHOTURE
NIZHNE-TAGILSKI
VERKHNE-TAGILSKI
ALAPAEVSKI

DAGO IS.
KRONSTADT
NARVA
ST. PETERSBURG

NOVGOROD

KHLYNOV
EKATERINBURG

OSEL IS.
TARTU (DERPT)
PSKOV
ALUKSNE
RIGA

YAROSLAVL

Tobol

W. Dvina

TVER
TROITSE-SERGIEV
MOSCOW
NIZHNI-NOVGOROD
KAZAN
UFA

P O L A N D

VILNA
GOLOVCHINO
Niemen
Pripet

SMOLENSK
Oka
DOBROE
TULA
LESNAYA

SIMBIRSK

SYZRAN
SAMARA
SARATOV
Yaik (Ural)

STARODUB
Desna
VORONEZH

YAITSKI GORODOK

KIEV
Dniepen
KHARKOV
POLTAVA
Donets
TSARITSYN
Volga

BRATSLAV
S. Bug
Dniester
Prut
KAMENNY ZATON
SECH
CHERKASSK
Don
KRASNY YAR

JASSY
BENDER
OCHAKOV
TAGANROG
AZOV
ASTRAKHAN

BRAILA
AZOV SEA
KERCH
Kuban
Terek
TERKI
TARKI
DERBENT

Danube
BAKHCHISARAY

B L A C K   S E A

C A S P I A N

ADRIANOPLE
CONSTANTINOPLE
Kura
BAKU

O T T O M A N   E M P I R E

RESHT

P E R S I A

MILES	0	100	200	400	600	800	1000

LEGEND

	AREA GAINED FROM TURKEY 1696 AND LOST TO TURKEY 1711
EUROPEAN RUSSIA, 1689	RUSSIAN BORDERS, 1725
ACQUISITIONS OF PETER I	OTHER BORDERS, 1725

the northern shore of the Gulf of Finland was even farther west than the original frontier established in 1323. This also was a turning point: never again were the Swedes able to annex Russian territory. Symbolic of Russia's new stature as a European power was Peter's adoption of the title "Emperor" in 1721.

The closing years of the reign witnessed a Russian invasion of Persia (1722–23), climaxed by the Russian annexation of the entire southern and western shores of the Caspian Sea, with the cities of Derbent and Baku. A few years after Peter's death, Russia voluntarily withdrew from most of these areas in order to secure Persian help in a new war with Turkey.

Peter's reign also saw Kamchatka and the Kurile Islands secured and additional gains in Central Asia (see below, page 54).

Map 18. Russia in Asia, 1689–1762

Territorial Changes in the East, 1689–1762

As noted above, Peter I's annexations along the Caspian littoral were transitory. In 1732 Russia voluntarily returned all lands south of the Kura River, and in 1735 she agreed to move the boundary north to the Sulak River (see above, Map 17). Nearly all of Russia's costly gains had been restored to Persia by 1735.

Elsewhere, however, the advance of Russia's frontiers was steady. In 1716 Omsk was founded on the middle Irtysh River; two years later Semipalatinsk was established far upstream (see Map 18). Meanwhile, the conquest of Kamchatka was proceeding, subsequent to its discovery (or possibly rediscovery) in 1697. By 1732 serious resistance from the natives had been checked, and in 1740 the naval base of Petropavlovsk was founded on the southeastern coast. At approximately the same time (beginning c. 1711), the Kurile Islands were being explored and claimed for Russia by venturesome Cossacks.

During the generally sterile reigns of the mediocre rulers who occupied the throne between the death of Peter I (1725) and the accession of Catherine II (1762), only minor changes were made in the map of the empire. In 1731 the Kazakhs of the Younger (or Lesser) Horde nominally accepted Russian sovereignty, thus extending Russian influence almost to the Aral Sea (see below, Map 25). About 1740 at least part of the Middle Horde also accepted Russian suzerainty, although Russia was not able to establish firm control over these Kazakhs until the nineteenth century.

Just north of the Kazakh territory, permanent gains were secured by the founding of Orsk (1735) and Orenburg (1743) on the Yaik River, renamed Ural River in 1775. The latter fort was used as a base for subsequent expeditions deep into Central Asia. Iletskaya Zashchita, a fort on the Ilek tributary of the Yaik, was also established in 1743. In 1752 another town named Petropavlovsk was founded, this one on the Ishim River.

54

LEGEND

ASIATIC (AND N. EUROPEAN) RUSSIA 1689

ANNEXATIONS IN ASIA 1689–1762

KAZAKH AREAS NOMINALLY RUSSIAN DEPENDENCIES FROM C. 1731–1740

RUSSIAN BOUNDARY IN ASIA 1762

0 100 200 400 600 800 1000

MILES

Meanwhile, the first Russians may have sighted Alaska in 1732, without realizing that they were viewing the North American mainland: Fedorov and Gvozdev supposedly reached the vicinity of Cape Prince of Wales, along the eastern shore of Bering Strait, in that year. More systematic expeditions followed: in 1741 Bering reached North America, and in 1743 the first of many merchant voyages to that fur-rich area was undertaken. The Aleutian Islands were also being explored at this time, during the two decades following their discovery in 1741. The stage was being set for ambitious Russian dreams and claims in North America during the following century (see below, pages 80–82).

Map 19. Russian Expansion in Europe, 1725–1762

The Reigns of Favorites and Foreigners

It is somewhat ironic that Peter the Great's weak successors had better fortune in battling the Turks than he experienced. In 1739, at the conclusion of four years of warfare, Russia regained Azov and both sides of the Don River estuary; but the Treaty of Belgrade prohibited Russian fortification of the area, as well as Russian shipping on the Azov or Black seas. More important strategically was the acquisition of part of the steppes, between the Southern Bug and the Don rivers, just north of the Crimean Tartar domain (see Map 19). This territory included all of Zaporozhie, but the Cossacks in that region retained a degree of autonomy until 1775, when their stronghold, New Sech, was destroyed. In order to increase Russian control in this turbulent area, two regiments of Serbs were settled on the right bank of the Dnieper River in 1752, and the area was known for a time as New Serbia. A few years later, additional Serbs were settled between the Dnieper and the Donets rivers, east of Zaporozhie.

The other lasting gain in Europe during this period was secured in 1743 (Treaty of Abo, also known as Turku), at the conclusion of a war which Sweden had launched in 1741 in an unsuccessful bid to recoup her losses of 1721. Although Cossack forces had occupied much of southern Finland, Russia annexed only a small portion in the southeast, just west and northwest of Vyborg. The frontier along the Gulf of Finland was then drawn along the Kymi River, the western limit of Novgorod's ancient sphere of influence (see above, Map 4).

As noted above (pages 52 and 54), this period also witnessed one of Russia's few voluntary cessions of territory: during the reign of Anna (1730–40) nearly all of the Caspian littoral won by Peter I was returned to Persia.

RUSSIAN EXPANSION IN EUROPE, 1725–1762

MAP 19

FINLAND

ABO
HELSINGFORS
FREDRIKSHAMN
VYBORG
TALLIN
ST. PETERSBURG
NOVGOROD
PSKOV
RIGA
MITAU
(JELGAVA)
POLOTSK
TVER
KOENIGSBERG
GROSS
JAEGERNDORF
GRODNO
SMOLENSK
MOSCOW
NIZHNI-
NOVGOROD
KAZAN
UFA
MINSK
BREST-
LITOVSK
LVOV
KIEV
VORONEZH
SAMARA
ORENBURG
ORSK
KHOTIN
BELGOROD
KHARKOV
NEW SERBIA
ZAPOROZHIE
TSARITSYN
JASSY
BENDER
OCHAKOV
NEW SECH
KINBURN
CHERKASSK
GUREV
PEREKOP
AZOV
ASTRAKHAN
BUCHAREST
CRIMEAN
KERCH
KHANATE
BAKHCHISARAY
Kuban
DERBENT
CONSTANTINOPLE
TBILISI
BAKU

BALTIC SEA
N. Dvina
W. Dvina
Bug
S. Bug
Dniester
Dnieper
Desna
Oka
Don
Donets
Volga
Kama
Yaik
Danube
Terek
Kura

BLACK SEA
CASPIAN SEA

OTTOMAN EMPIRE
POLAND
PERSIA

| 0 | 100 | 200 | 400 | 600 | 800 | 1000 |

MILES

LEGEND

EUROPEAN (AND W. SIBERIAN)
RUSSIA 1725

ANNEXATIONS IN
EUROPE 1725–1762

PERSIAN TERRITORY
HELD BY RUSSIA 1723 – 1735

RUSSIAN BOUNDARY
IN EUROPE 1762

OTHER BOUNDARIES 1762

Map 20. European Russia, 1762–1796

The Annexations of Catherine II

If successful aggression be the mark of greatness, Catherine II (1762–96) earned her sobriquet, "the Great." She subjugated the Crimean Tartars, engineered the extinction of the Polish nation, began the conquest of the Caucasus (see below, pages 72–74), extended Russian territory in Central Asia (see Map 25), annexed the Aleutian Islands, and authorized the first Russian settlement in Alaska (see page 80).

The most significant of these acquisitions were those at Poland's expense. By the first partition in 1772, undertaken jointly with Prussia and Austria, Russia annexed the White Russian areas of Polotsk, Vitebsk, and Mogilev, in addition to part of Lithuania. The new frontier gave Russia the entire right bank of the Western Dvina River, as well as the entire left bank of the Dnieper. By the second partition in 1793, effected jointly with Prussia, Russia acquired the White Russian area of Minsk and also right bank Ukraine (the Ukraine west of the Dnieper). In contrast to the third partition in 1795, the first two could be justified on ethnic and historic grounds: the entire area had been part of Kievan Rus. However, by the third partition, in which all three of Poland's aggressive neighbors again participated, Russia acquired—in addition to the last parts of White Russia—Kurland and the remainder of Lithuania—areas which had never been Russian. Technically, Kurland voluntarily accepted Russian rule when the last Duke, Peter Biron, abdicated the throne in 1795. Russian influence had been predominant in the Duchy intermittently since 1737, and consistently since 1763, although Kurland nominally remained a fief of Poland. For the first time in her history, Russia now had common borders with Prussia and Austria. Her western frontier followed stretches of the Niemen, Bug (Western), and Dniester rivers.

In two victorious wars with the Turks, Catherine annexed most of the northern shore of the Black Sea. The Treaty of Kuchuk-Kainardzhi (1774) gave Russia her first foothold directly on the coast, between the

EUROPEAN RUSSIA, 1762–1796

MAP 20

LEGEND

MILES

0 100 200 400 600 800 1000

EUROPEAN (AND W.
SIBERIAN) RUSSIA 1762

ANNEXED TO RUSSIA BY
PARTITIONS OF POLAND:

1ST. 1772   2ND. 1793   3RD. 1795

ANNEXED 1774 (TREATY OF
KUCHUK–KAINARDZHI)

ANNEXED 1783 (CRIMEA)

ANNEXED 1791
(TREATY OF JASSY)

ANNEXED C. 1786 (TARKI)

RUSSIAN BOUNDARY IN
EUROPE 1796

OTHER BOUNDARIES 1796

Southern Bug and the Dnieper rivers, including the port of Kherson. At the same time, the 1739 restrictions on fortifying the Azov area were removed, and Russia acquired important political and economic rights within the Ottoman Empire. Furthermore, the Crimea was declared independent from Turkey, and Russia annexed the ports of Kerch and Enikale in the eastern part of that peninsula. Finally, the treaty awarded the Kabarda area (northern Caucasus; see Map 24) to Russia, although Russian control there remained tenuous until the nineteenth century.

To no one's surprise, the "independence" of the Crimean Tartars in 1774 was followed by the formal annexation of their state, under strong Russian pressure, in 1783. This coup gave Russia both sides of the Sea of Azov, to the Kuban River in the southeast. It ended centuries of conflict with the Crimean descendants of Batu's Mongols.

Following a new war with the Turks, the Treaty of Jassy in 1791 (1792 by the calendar in use in the West) confirmed Russia's annexation of the Crimea; it also awarded Russia the northwestern Black Sea littoral, between the Southern Bug and the Dniester rivers, including the ports of Ochakov and Gadzhibei, the latter being renamed Odessa. Catherine had succeeded where even Peter I had failed: she had made Russia a Black Sea power, with a fleet to prove it. Further action against the Ottoman Empire was forestalled only by her death.

Catherine's eventful reign had witnessed the annexation of approximately 200,000 square miles of territory, though millions of the inhabitants remained hostile to Russian rule.

Map 21. Mediterranean Outposts, 1798–1807

Early Russian Relations with Napoleonic France

For a very brief period in her history, between 1798 and the Tilsit agreement of 1807, Russia was a de facto Mediterranean power. This period was also unique in another respect: for the first time Russia was allied (from 1798 to 1805) with her ancient enemy, the Ottoman Empire. Ironically, although England was also allied with Russia at that time in the Second Coalition against Napoleon, it was England that prevented Russia from regaining military access to the Mediterranean.

During the winter of 1798–99 a joint Russo-Turkish fleet under the command of Admiral Ushakov drove the French from the Ionian Islands, which France had seized from Venice in 1797. In 1800 the islands (Corfu, Paxo, Leucas, Ithaca, Zante, Cephalonia, and Cythera) were organized into the "Septinsular Republic," which was formally under Turkish suzerainty but actually garrisoned by Russian forces. (Russian naval forces had also engaged the French in Egypt in 1798 and in Italy in 1799.)

In 1806 a Russian force from Corfu occupied the Dalmatian port of Kotor (Cattaro), which France had acquired from Austria the previous year.

By the terms of the Peace of Tilsit in 1807, Russia transferred both Kotor and the Ionian Islands to France. Although French control did not last beyond the Napoleonic era, Russia never regained these strategic footholds in the Mediterranean. In fact England, while united with Russia against Napoleon, had been checking Russian ambitions in the area. For example, although Paul I had accepted the title of Grand Master of the Maltese Order in 1798, a few months after the French had occupied their island, in 1799 a Russian fleet was prevented by the British from attacking the French garrison. In 1800 the British themselves attacked and occupied Malta.

Only the exigencies of the Napoleonic upheaval permitted Russia to gain even a brief foothold in the Mediterranean; the same factors caused her to lose those strategic and potentially most significant bases.

64

MEDITERRANEAN OUTPOSTS, 1798–1807

MAP 21

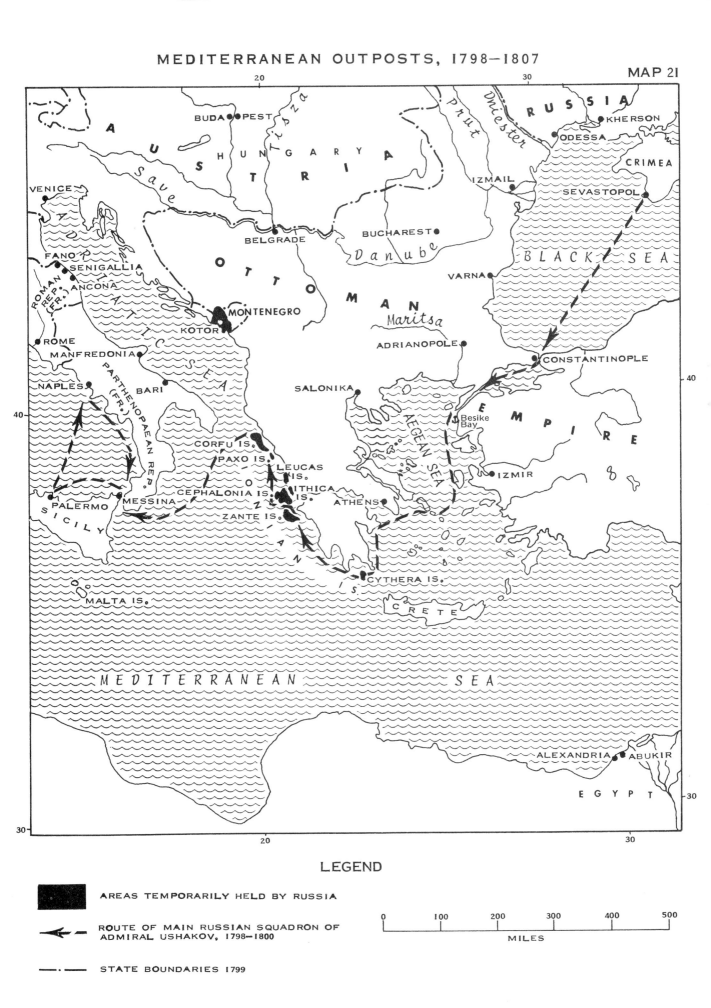

LEGEND

AREAS TEMPORARILY HELD BY RUSSIA

ROUTE OF MAIN RUSSIAN SQUADRON OF
ADMIRAL USHAKOV, 1798–1800

STATE BOUNDARIES 1799

| 0 | 100 | 200 | 300 | 400 | 500 |

MILES

Map 22. European Russia, 1796–1815

Later Russian Relations with Napoleonic France

Tilsit was not a complete loss for Russia; the Belostok area, which had been Prussian since the third partition of Poland, was ceded to Russia by a victorious France. Two years later, in 1809, Napoleon also presented to Russia the Tarnopol area in eastern Galicia, which Austria had acquired in the first Polish partition. However, Tarnopol was returned to Austria in 1815.

While the Tilsit agreement was still in effect, Russia invaded Swedish Finland in 1808. As a result, the entire Grand Duchy of Finland (to the Tornio and Muonio rivers) and the Aaland Islands were annexed by Russia in 1809. This large area remained part of the Empire, with varying degrees of autonomy, until 1917. At the beginning of 1812, only months before Napoleon's invasion of Russia, the Tsar granted a revision of the boundaries of the Grand Duchy to the 1617 line north of Lake Ladoga and to a point approximately twenty miles from St. Petersburg west of that lake. This somewhat unprecedented gesture meant that Vyborg, the western part of the Karelian Isthmus, and the area north of Lake Ladoga were restored to the Finns—remaining, of course, part of the Russian Empire. In 1833 the northeastern boundary of the Grand Duchy—from the Barents Sea to a point just south of 64° N. Latitude—was also relocated eastward. These changes assumed more significance later when Finland achieved independence.

The Treaty of Bucharest, signed at the conclusion of a new war with Turkey (1806–12), gave the Russians Bessarabia, which lies between the Dniester and the Prut rivers. (For a detailed map of Bessarabia see below, Map 23.) At the same time, Turkey recognized Russia's annexation of western Georgia, and the next year Persia made sizable concessions to Russia. (For details on the Caucasus region, see below, page 74.)

By the Vienna settlement in 1815, which marked the end of the Napoleonic era, Russia acquired most of the former Grand Duchy of Warsaw, the French-dominated buffer state on her Polish frontier. For

EUROPEAN RUSSIA, 1796—1815

MAP 22

ARCTIC OCEAN

BARENTS SEA

Muonio
Tornio

TORNIO
ULEABORG
ARKHANGELSK

UMEA
VASA
N. Dvina

TAMMERFORS
AALAND IS.
ABO
HELSINGFORS
VYBORG
PETROZAVODSK

STOCKHOLM

S W E D E N

L. LADOGA
ST. PETERSBURG

B A L T I C   S E A

TALLIN
NOVGOROD
VOLOGDA
VYATKA
PERM

RIGA
PSKOV
KOSTROMA
YAROSLAVL

MITAU
(JELGAVA)
W. Dvina
TVER

TILSIT
VLADIMIR
NIZHNI—
NOVGOROD
KAZAN

KOENIGSBERG
KOVNO
VITEBSK
BORODINO
MOSCOW

STETTIN
DANZIG
VILNA
SMOLENSK
MALOYAROSLAVETS

P R U S S I A
SUVALKI
STUDYANKA
KRASNY
KALUGA

GRODNO
MINSK
Berezina
TULA
Don
PENZA
SAMARA

BELOSTOK
Niemen
MOGILEV
OREL
ORENBURG

WARSAW
RADOM
LUBLIN
CHERNIGOV
KURSK
TAMBOV
Ural

Vistula
ZHITOMIR
KIEV
VORONEZH
SARATOV

AUSTERLITZ
LVOV
TARNOPOL
KHARKOV
TSARITSYN

A U S T R I A
Tisza
Prut
Dniester
Dnieper
POLTAVA
GUREV
Volga

BUDA
PEST
Danube
EKATERINOSLAV

JASSY
KISHINEV
BENDER
TAGANROG
NOVOCHERKASSK

BELGRADE
KHERSON
AZOV
ASTRAKHAN
CASPIAN SEA

O T T O M A N   E M P I R E
BUCHAREST
IZMAIL
ODESSA
PEREKOP
EKATERINODAR
Kuban
STAVROPOL

NIKOPOL
RUSE
CONSTANTSA
SIMFEROPOL
SEVASTOPOL

MILES

0   100   200   400   600   800   1000

LEGEND

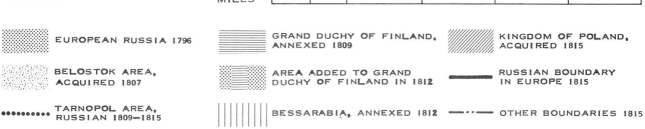

EUROPEAN RUSSIA 1796

GRAND DUCHY OF FINLAND, ANNEXED 1809

KINGDOM OF POLAND, ACQUIRED 1815

BELOSTOK AREA, ACQUIRED 1807

AREA ADDED TO GRAND DUCHY OF FINLAND IN 1812

RUSSIAN BOUNDARY IN EUROPE 1815

TARNOPOL AREA, RUSSIAN 1809—1815

BESSARABIA, ANNEXED 1812

OTHER BOUNDARIES 1815

the first time in history, Russia then controlled the central Vistula basin and the city of Warsaw. This Kingdom of Poland (informally termed "Congress Poland"), which was united to the Russian crown by personal union, enjoyed considerable local autonomy until the unsuccessful Polish revolution of 1830–31.

By the end of the Napoleonic era Russia was the predominant military power on the Continent, and had extended her borders deep into Central Europe and Scandinavia.

Map 23. Bessarabia and the Danube Delta, Nineteenth Century

A Century of Relatively Stable Western Borders

In contrast to her considerable expansion in the Caucasus, Central Asia, and the Far East (see below, Maps 24, 25, and 27), Russia's European boundaries remained relatively stable in the century between the Congress of Vienna and the First World War. The minor exceptions were all the result of wars with Turkey.

By the Peace of Adrianople in 1829, Russia acquired the Danube River delta (i.e. the three mouths of the Danube—the Kiliya, Sulina, and St. George channels; see Map 23), as well as territory in the Caucasus and the eastern Black Sea region (see page 74). One consequence of the humiliating defeat in the Crimean War was the return in 1856 of the Danubian delta to Turkey; another result was the transfer of the three southern districts of Bessarabia to the principality of Moldavia, which became part of the new state of Rumania after its union with Wallachia in 1859 (officially in 1862).

Southern Bessarabia was returned to Russia by the terms of the treaties of San Stefano and Berlin in 1878; however, Rumania was compensated by the Danubian delta and most of the Dobrudzha, which lies due south of the lower Danube. Russia's southwestern boundary remained on the left bank of the Kiliya mouth of the Danube until the First World War.

As a result of these alternating changes in the southwest, Russia's western frontiers in 1914 were the same as those of 1815 (see above, Map 22).

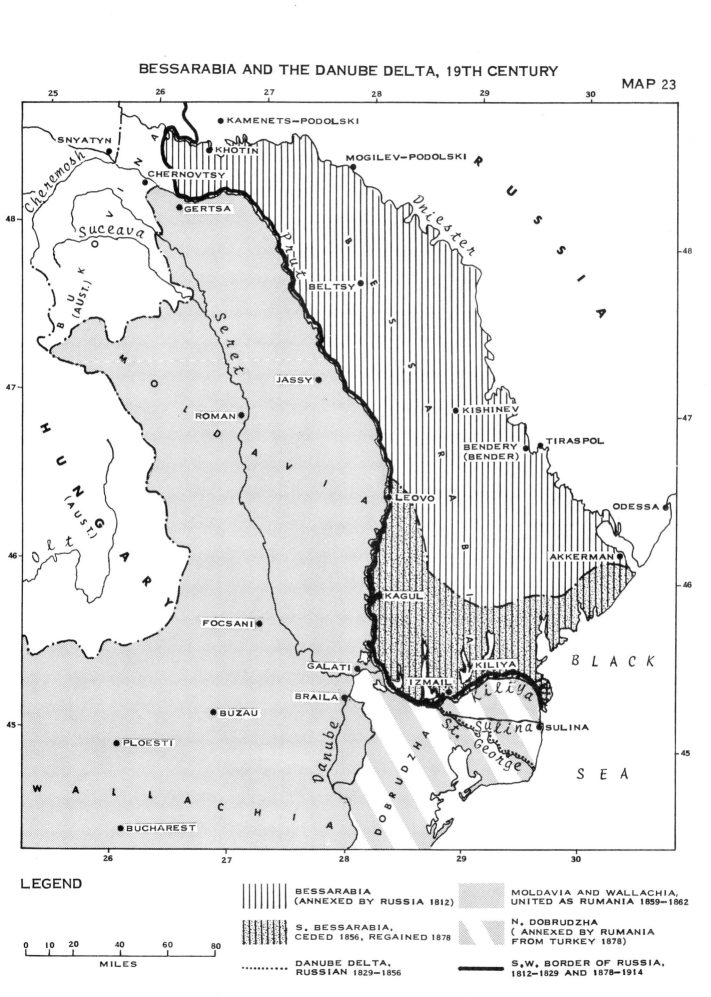

BESSARABIA AND THE DANUBE DELTA, 19TH CENTURY

MAP 23

SNYATYN
Cheremosh
KAMENETS-PODOLSKI
KHOTIN
CHERNOVTSY
MOGILEV-PODOLSKI
RUSSIA
Dniester
GERTSA
Suceava
(AUST.)
BUKOVINA
Prut
BELTSY
BESSARABIA
Seret
JASSY
ROMAN
KISHINEV
MOLDAVIA
BENDERY
(BENDER)
TIRASPOL
HUNGARY
(AUST.)
Olt
LEOVO
ODESSA
AKKERMAN
KAGUL
FOCSANI
BLACK
GALATI
KILIYA
BRAILA
IZMAIL
Kiliya
Danube
BUZAU
DOBRUDZHA
St. George
Sulina
SULINA
PLOESTI
SEA
WALLACHIA
BUCHAREST

LEGEND

BESSARABIA (ANNEXED BY RUSSIA 1812)	MOLDAVIA AND WALLACHIA, UNITED AS RUMANIA 1859—1862
S. BESSARABIA, CEDED 1856, REGAINED 1878	N. DOBRUDZHA (ANNEXED BY RUMANIA FROM TURKEY 1878)
DANUBE DELTA, RUSSIAN 1829—1856	S.W. BORDER OF RUSSIA, 1812—1829 AND 1878—1914

0 10 20   40   60   80

MILES

Map 24. The Caucasus and Transcaucasia, 1763–1914

Conquest of the Caucasus and Transcaucasia

Russia had reached the Terek River and Kabarda, just north of the Caucasus, in the sixteenth century (see above, page 38), but the subjugation of the areas between the Black and Caspian seas was not completed until 1878. Most of this area was conquered during the course of approximately one century, between 1783 and 1878. The annexations were not simply a north–south movement; the more accessible coastal regions and Transcaucasia, except for the southwestern corner held by Turkey, succumbed long before the rugged northern mountain areas were pacified. However, dissension among the heterogeneous native peoples and pressures from their oppressive Turkish and Persian neighbors facilitated Russia's early acquisition of part of the central mountain region, namely Georgia.

As noted above (page 62), Turkey ceded the Kabarda region to Russia in 1774. However, serious inroads into Greater Kabarda did not begin until 1791, and despite some pro-Russian sentiment the area was not firmly united with Russia until about 1825. The adjoining Osetia region came under partial Russian control in 1774; it was finally annexed in 1806.

Meanwhile, Russians had moved south from the vicinity of Mozdok, founded in 1763 near the territory of the friendly Little Kabardans, and had established contact with Georgia via the Daryal gorge on the upper Terek River. Midway between Mozdok and the Daryal Pass they founded Vladikavkaz (1784), which served as the northern terminal of the Georgian Military Road leading to Tiflis (Tbilisi). A Russian expedition had reached Georgia via this route in 1769, when Russia and Georgia were allied against Turkey. In 1783 Eastern Georgia (Kartlia and Kakhetia) voluntarily accepted Russian protection; in 1801, fearing a Persian invasion, the kingdom accepted formal incorporation into the Empire. Thereafter Russian domination of most of the disunited western states

THE CAUCASUS AND TRANSCAUCASIA, 1763–1914

MAP 24

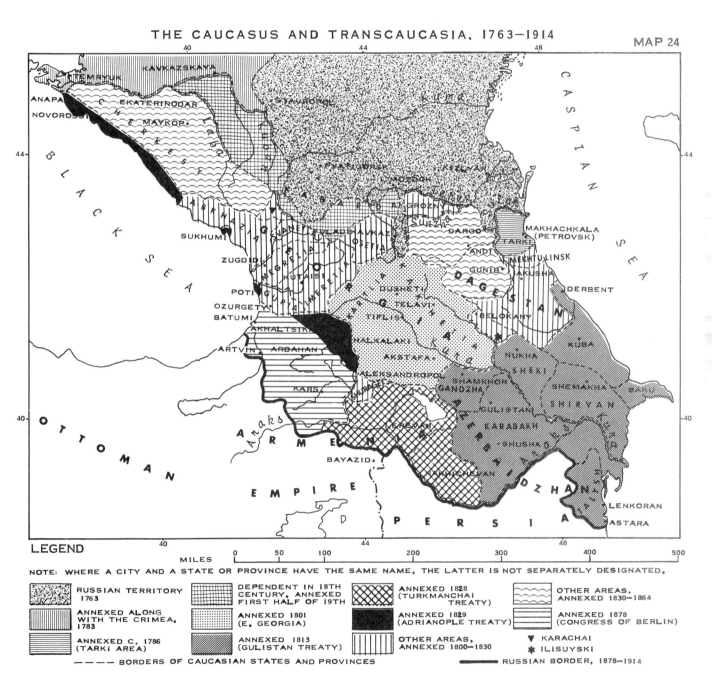

LEGEND

NOTE: WHERE A CITY AND A STATE OR PROVINCE HAVE THE SAME NAME, THE LATTER IS NOT SEPARATELY DESIGNATED.

RUSSIAN TERRITORY 1763

ANNEXED ALONG WITH THE CRIMEA, 1783

ANNEXED C. 1786 (TARKI AREA)

DEPENDENT IN 18TH CENTURY, ANNEXED FIRST HALF OF 19TH

ANNEXED 1801 (E. GEORGIA)

ANNEXED 1813 (GULISTAN TREATY)

ANNEXED 1828 (TURKMANCHAI TREATY)

ANNEXED 1829 (ADRIANOPLE TREATY)

OTHER AREAS, ANNEXED 1800–1830

OTHER AREAS, ANNEXED 1830–1864

ANNEXED 1878 (CONGRESS OF BERLIN)

▼ KARACHAI

✴ ILISUYSKI

— — — BORDERS OF CAUCASIAN STATES AND PROVINCES

——— RUSSIAN BORDER, 1878–1914

which had once been part of ancient Georgia followed rapidly. Again Russia advanced in two steps; de facto annexation in the guise of a protectorate preceded de jure annexation. (Dates in parentheses are for the latter.) The principality of Megrelia (Mingrelia) came under Russian control in 1803 (1867); in 1804 the kingdom of Imeretia (1810) and the principality of Guria (1829), also c. 1804 the principality of Svanetia (1858); and the principality of Abkhazia in 1810 (1864).

Persia tried to counter these inroads into her sphere of influence, but she lost the war with Russia which followed (1804–13). By the Treaty of Gulistan, Persia not only acknowledged Russian control of Georgia, but also ceded Dagestan and northern Azerbaidzhan. Russia had conquered the latter area piecemeal: the khanate of Gandzha in 1804; the khanates of Karabakh, Shirvan, and Sheki in 1805; the khanates of Kuba, Baku, and Derbent in 1806; and the Talysh khanate (the extreme southern portion of Russia's western Caspian coastline) in 1813. In 1805 Russia also acquired the Shuragel region from Persia.

Meanwhile, the ruler of the Caspian Sea coast south of the Sulak River, the Shamkhal of Tarki, had become a Russian vassal around 1786. By the turn of the century, the small Mekhtulinsk khanate, just to the south, had also come under Russian rule. The native town of Tarki was subsequently overshadowed by the adjacent port of Petrovsk —the modern Makhachkala—which was founded in 1844.

In 1817 Russia's border was pushed south from the middle Terek to the Sunzha River, where a new military line was established; the Groznaya fortress (modern Grozny) was founded there in 1818.

Although Persia had ceded Dagestan in 1813, the southern part of this rugged area was not subdued until about 1821 (the Dzharo-Belokany region and the Ilisuyski sultanate in the west were not formally annexed until 1830), and the northern regions were not pacified until 1859.

The Treaty of Turkmanchai, terminating a new war with Persia (1826–28), awarded Russia the eastern Armenian khanates of Erevan and Nakhichevan. The major portion of the Russo-Persian border in Transcaucasia then followed the Araks (Araxes) River. Except for a small Russian bridgehead across that river near Nakhichevan, which was returned to Persia in 1893, and minor rectifications connected with demarcation in the 1950s, Russia's 430-odd-mile boundary with Persia west of the Caspian Sea has not changed since 1828.

By the Treaty of Adrianople in 1829, Turkey ceded the Akhaltsikh province, which was reunited with Georgia. The same treaty awarded Russia the entire northeastern littoral of the Black Sea, with the ports of Anapa, Sukhumi, and Poti. The latter two had been retained by the Turks when Russia annexed their hinterland between 1803 and 1810.

A year earlier the Russians had annexed the small Karachai area southwest of the headwaters of the Kuban River. The adjacent region in the northwest, lying mainly between the Black Sea littoral wrested from Turkey in 1829 and the Kuban and Laba rivers, was gradually subjugated between 1830 and 1864. This was the land of the Cherkesy (Adyge), who had become Russian vassals three centuries earlier (see above, page 38).

The final gains in Transcaucasia resulted from the Russo-Turkish War of 1877–78. The abortive Treaty of San Stefano awarded Russia the districts of Batumi, Kars, Ardahan, and Bayazid (Bayazet). The Congress of Berlin confirmed most of these acquisitions, except that the Bayazid area was restored to Turkey and Batumi was termed a free port under Russian control. With this settlement, the Russian borders in Transcaucasia remained virtually stable until the First World War.

Map 25. Expansion in Central Asia, 1763–1914

The Conquest of Kazakhstan and Turkestan

In 1763 Russia annexed a small area east of Semipalatinsk which included the headwaters of the Ob River (see Map 25). For nearly a century thereafter, all her Asiatic acquisitions were in the regions west and southwest of that area.

As noted above (page 54), Russia established nominal sovereignty over the Lesser and Middle Kazakh Hordes in the fourth decade of the eighteenth century; however, firm control over these nomadic tribes was not secured until about 1822. When the Elder Horde was also subjugated (c. 1847), the Uzbek rulers to the south of the Kazakh areas found themselves face to face with the Russian Empire for the first time. In a bitter struggle lasting three decades, each of these heterogeneous and weak states (Kokand, Bukhara, and Khiva) succumbed to Russian domination.

Because much of the area was desert wasteland, it was necessary for the Russians to capture or establish advanced bases for the conquest of the Uzbek territory. In 1853 Ak-Mechet in northwestern Kokand was seized (and renamed Perovsk); the next year the fortress Verny (Alma-Ata) was founded on the site of a Kazakh settlement, just beyond the northeastern frontier. A decade later, the conquest of the khanate was undertaken in earnest: Chimkent fell in 1864, and in 1865 the capital at Tashkent was successfully stormed. By the terms of the peace treaty of 1868, Kokand became a protectorate, but a subsequent revolt led to Russia's outright annexation of the entire khanate in 1876.

Meanwhile, Bukhara's forces had attacked the Russians in Kokand in 1865, initiating a war which resulted in their loss of Samarkand and their capital, Bukhara, in 1868. The peace concluded that same year provided for Russia's annexation of Samarkand and adjacent areas; the remainder of the emirate of Bukhara became a Russian protectorate, a status it retained until 1917.

The khanate of Khiva, the least accessible of the Uzbek states, was

EXPANSION IN CENTRAL ASIA, 1763–1914

MAP 25

LEGEND

|||||||| RUSSIAN TERRITORY 1762

OB HEADWATERS, ANNEXED 1763

PREDOMINANTLY KAZAKH TERRITORY, ANNEXED 1801–1855

UZBEK TERRITORY, ANNEXED 1853–1885 (INCLUDES TURKMEN REGIONS IN W AND SW)

PROTECTORATE OF BUKHARA, 1868–1917

PROTECTORATE OF KHIVA, 1873–1917

KULDZHA REGION, OCCUPIED BY RUSSIA 1871–1881

ANNEXATIONS IN LAKE ZAYSAN REGION:
1864   1881

PAMIR REGION, ANNEXED 1895

——— RUSSIAN BOUNDARY 1895–1914

—·— OTHER BOUNDARIES 1914

MILES 0 100 200 400 600 800 1000

the last to fall. Russian preparations for the campaign were completed in 1873, and the capital, Khiva, was soon captured. By the terms of the peace concluded that year, Russia annexed the right bank of Khiva's sector of the Amu-Darya River. The remainder of the khanate, like neighboring Bukhara, remained a Russian protectorate until 1917.

In 1869 a Russo-Persian agreement had established the lower Atrek River as their common boundary east of the Caspian Sea. In 1873 Russian forces occupied the mostly uninhabited southeastern littoral of the Caspian as far south as the Atrek. All of the annexed Uzbek areas mentioned above were incorporated into the governor-generalship of Turkestan, centered at Tashkent, which had been established in 1867.

Between 1881 and 1885 Russia conquered the isolated Teke Turkmen settlements south of the Kara-Kum Desert, which had been under the intermittent control of Khiva and Bukhara. In 1881 Geok-Tepe fell; in 1884 Merv (Mary) succumbed; and finally, in 1885, the Afghan border area around Kushka was annexed.

These advances were accompanied by new agreements with Persia; conventions signed in 1881 and 1893 delimited their border eastward, the latter to the Afghan tripoint. Except for minor changes in 1921 and 1954, the 600-odd-mile Russo-Persian boundary east of the Caspian has remained constant since the late nineteenth century.

Afghanistan, another party directly interested in the Russian advance in Central Asia, was not even formally consulted by her new neighbor until 1921 (and again in 1946). Instead, the British negotiated agreements with the Russians (1873, 1885, and 1895) and with the Afghans (1893) which delimited the Russo-Afghan border. To date, only minor rectifications have changed those British-made boundaries. For 800 of its approximately 1,281 miles, the border follows the Amu-Darya and two of its headstreams, the Pyandzh and the Pamir.

In 1895 Imperial Russia made her last significant addition of contiguous territory, which was also the closest point in Russia to British India. This was the rugged Pamir section, separated from India by the panhandle of Afghanistan, which is only ten miles wide in places.

Meanwhile, northeast of the Uzbek areas, Russia had made some minor additions to her borders. In 1864 she annexed the area north and

78

south of Lake Zaysan and part of the left bank of the Black Irtysh River. The military post of Zaysan was founded southeast of the lake in 1868. The lower right bank of the Black Irtysh, opposite the territory seized in 1864, was annexed in 1881 by agreement with China.

In 1871 Russian forces occupied the Kuldzha region along the upper Ili River, part of Chinese Turkestan. The ensuing diplomatic dispute was settled in 1881 by the Treaty of St. Petersburg (or Ili). Russia withdrew from most of the contested area in exchange for the territory along the right bank of the Black Irtysh mentioned above.

These acquisitions of vast areas inhabited by millions of non-Slavic peoples made Russia a major colonial power, even though she was simultaneously yielding much of her overseas empire, as Map 26 illustrates.

Map 26. Russia in the North Pacific, Eighteenth–Nineteenth Centuries

Russian Possessions in the North Pacific and in North America

Captain Bering, a Danish navigator in the Russian service, discovered the strait separating Asia from America which bears his name, the Diomede Islands which divide the strait, and St. Lawrence Island in 1728. In 1741 he also led the first Russian expedition which is definitely known to have landed personnel in the vicinity of Alaska (although at least one Russian ship may have previously reached the area; see above, page 56). A party from his ship spent a few hours on Kayak Island, while other landing parties from the ship of his subordinate, Lt. Chirikov, were sent ashore, and disappeared forever in the Alexander Archipelago, probably on Baranof Island. On his return voyage that same year, Bering discovered the Komandorski Islands, approximately 110 miles east of central Kamchatka. Bering and Medny islands are the largest of this group, which Russia still retains. (See Insert B, Map 26.)

The news of the abundant furs available in the Aleutian Islands, also discovered by Bering's expedition in 1741, sparked Russian interest in Alaska, which was to persist for a century and a quarter. By 1766 all of the Aleutian Islands had been explored and the natives brutally suppressed. Two decades later (1786–87), the Pribilof (Seal) Islands were discovered, and the wasteful slaughter of the seals began.

In 1784 the merchant Shelekhov established the first permanent Russian settlement in Alaska, Old Kodiak at Three Saints Bay on the southeastern shore of Kodiak Island; in 1792 this colony was moved to the more favorable site of the present town of Kodiak on the northern coast of the island.

From the time of the first merchant voyage to the Aleutians in 1745 until 1799 there was fierce competition among Russian traders in Alaska, coupled with haphazard exploration and settlement on private initiative. However, in 1799 the Russian American Company was chartered, with

RUSSIA IN THE NORTH PACIFIC, 18TH–19TH CENTURIES

MAP 26

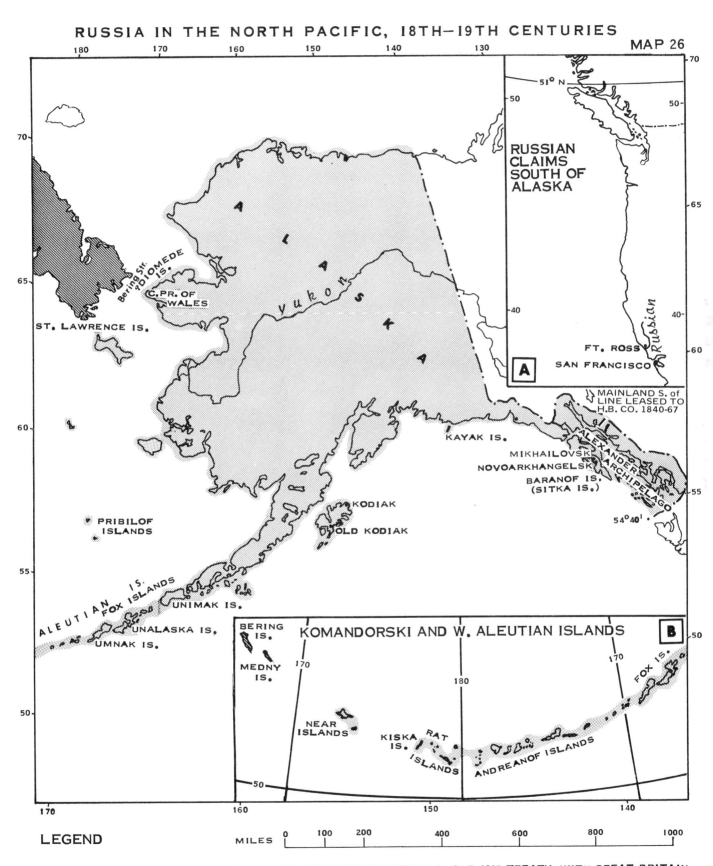

A — RUSSIAN CLAIMS SOUTH OF ALASKA

FT. ROSS
SAN FRANCISCO
Russian
51° N
54° 40'

MAINLAND S. of LINE LEASED TO H.B. CO. 1840-67

A L A S K A

Yukon

Bering Str.
DIOMEDE IS.
C. PR. OF WALES
ST. LAWRENCE IS.

KAYAK IS.

MIKHAILOVSK
NOVOARKHANGELSK
BARANOF IS.
(SITKA IS.)
ALEXANDER ARCHIPELAGO

KODIAK
OLD KODIAK

PRIBILOF ISLANDS

ALEUTIAN IS.
FOX ISLANDS
UNIMAK IS.
UNALASKA IS.
UMNAK IS.

B — KOMANDORSKI AND W. ALEUTIAN ISLANDS

BERING IS.
MEDNY IS.
NEAR ISLANDS
KISKA IS.
RAT ISLANDS
ANDREANOF ISLANDS
FOX IS.

LEGEND

MILES 0 100 200 400 600 800 1000

— · — LIMIT OF RUSSIAN CLAIMS PER 1824 TREATY WITH U.S. AND 1825 TREATY WITH GREAT BRITAIN

AREA SOLD TO U.S. 1867   RUSSIAN TERRITORY AFTER 1867

monopolistic privileges, government support, and virtually unlimited authority over all territory north of 55° N. Latitude, plus the Aleutian, Pribilof, Diomede, and other islands. Mikhailovsk, the first Russian colony on Baranof Island, then known as Sitka Island, was founded that same year. After rebellious natives wiped out Mikhailovsk in 1802, their village six miles to the south was bombarded (1804), and on its site the new town of Novoarkhangelsk, later called Sitka, was established. In 1805 this new settlement became the headquarters for the Company's operations in North America.

Grandiose projects were envisioned by the Company, whose charter empowered it to discover and occupy new territories for Russia. Its agents tried in vain to secure a foothold in the Hawaiian Islands in the first two decades of the century. They were somewhat more successful in California, where they founded a colony a few miles north of the Russian River, not far from San Francisco. Begun in 1811, the settlement was formally established the next year as Ft. Ross (see Insert A, Map 26). Designed as a lever against Spanish interests and as a granary for Sitka and other northern posts, the fort was a failure in both respects. In 1841 this most advanced outpost of Russian America was sold to John Sutter.

The Company never succeeded in establishing any viable, self-sufficient colonies. Its energies were devoted mainly to the exploitation of the natives for furs, and its operations were generally confined to the coastal areas. Consequently, Russian America never had a significant population or a strong defensive base; Russian control was always tenuous and highly vulnerable.

The Company increasingly became a government agency (after 1821 it was virtually run by naval officers), and its commercial position deteriorated. For the last 27 years of its existence (1840–67), the Company even leased half of the mainland panhandle (from Cape Spencer south) to the rival Hudson's Bay Company for an annual rent. When its third twenty-year charter expired in 1862, the Company was almost bankrupt; it was subsequently maintained on a temporary basis for purely political reasons.

From the mid-1850s the sale of Alaska had been under consideration.

Besides the declining revenues, the Russians had other reasons to view the area as a liability. Russia could not hope to defend her weak American possessions in the event that England or the United States should attack them, and there had been long-standing friction with both nations in the area. The Monroe Doctrine was issued in 1823 partially in response to an 1821 Russian edict which had claimed exclusive navigation rights above 51° N. Latitude and 100 miles out to sea. That dispute was settled in 1824 by a treaty limiting Russian claims to 54°40′ N. and providing for free navigation and trading privileges on a reciprocal basis. In 1825 England and Russia finally described, in rather misleading terms, the boundary between Alaska and British Canada, and similar trading privileges were exchanged (see Map 26). In 1835, when both treaties had expired, Russia attempted to prevent foreign vessels from approaching the coast north of 54°40′. However, freebooting traders, whalers, and prospectors habitually ignored the niceties of boundary and trade agreements.

Finally, the Crimean War dramatized the vulnerability of Russia's Pacific possessions. Russia's hasty defensive expedients consisted of a fictitious transfer of the Company's properties to an American firm and a neutrality agreement between the British Hudson's Bay Company and the Russian American Company. In 1855 an Anglo-French squadron in the North Pacific bombarded Petropavlovsk in Kamchatka, but Alaska was not attacked. Russia concluded that it would be better to have America control the region than to see it fall to its archenemy, England.

For these reasons, the Russian government sold the entire area (Alaska, the Aleutian, St. Lawrence, Little Diomede, and Pribilof islands) to the United States in 1867. Since then, the boundary between the United States and Russia has passed through the Bering Strait between Big and Little Diomede islands (Russian and American respectively), which are less than five miles apart. Russia had wisely cut her losses and avoided an imperialistic war in North America; by following a different policy in Asia, she was destined to become involved in just such a war with Japan (see below, page 88).

Map 27. The Russian Far East, 1763–1897

Acquisition of Sakhalin, the Amur, and the Maritime Province

There were no changes in the mainland boundaries of the Russian Far East from about 1732, when Kamchatka was finally subjugated, until the annexation of the Amur River basin in the latter half of the following century; the beginning date for Map 27 is thus only for continuity—it resumes where Map 18 terminates.

In 1853 Captain Nevelskoy, on behalf of the Russian American Company, led a military expedition to Sakhalin Island. Since the Japanese had previously settled there, an agreement for joint administration was concluded in 1855. About the same time, the Japanese secured the southern islands of the Kurile chain; by agreement in 1855 the division of Russo-Japanese spheres of influence was the Vries (Friz) Strait between Urup and Iturup islands. However, continuing Russian pressure against the Japanese on Sakhalin culminated in the Treaty of St. Petersburg (1875), by which Japan ceded all of Sakhalin Island to Russia in exchange for the northern Kuriles, giving Japan control of all the Kurile Islands.

While sowing the seeds of future conflict with Japan, Russia was simultaneously renewing earlier friction with China. As noted above (page 48), Russia had been excluded from the Amur valley by the Treaty of Nerchinsk in 1689. Nevertheless, in 1850 the aggressive Governor-General of Eastern Siberia, N. Muravev, using the Russian American Company as a thin cover, established the post of Nikolaevsk a few miles above the Amur estuary. In 1856 the military post of Ust-Zeisk, renamed Blagoveshchensk in 1858, was founded at the confluence of the Zeya and Amur rivers; two years later the town of Khabarovsk was built on the middle Amur.

In the same year, while the Chinese were preoccupied with Anglo-French attacks, they were pressured into signing the Treaty of Aigun, by which Russia acquired the left bank of the Amur from the Argun River to the sea, plus joint control of the area between the Ussuri River and

84

MAP 27

THE RUSSIAN FAR EAST, 1763–1897

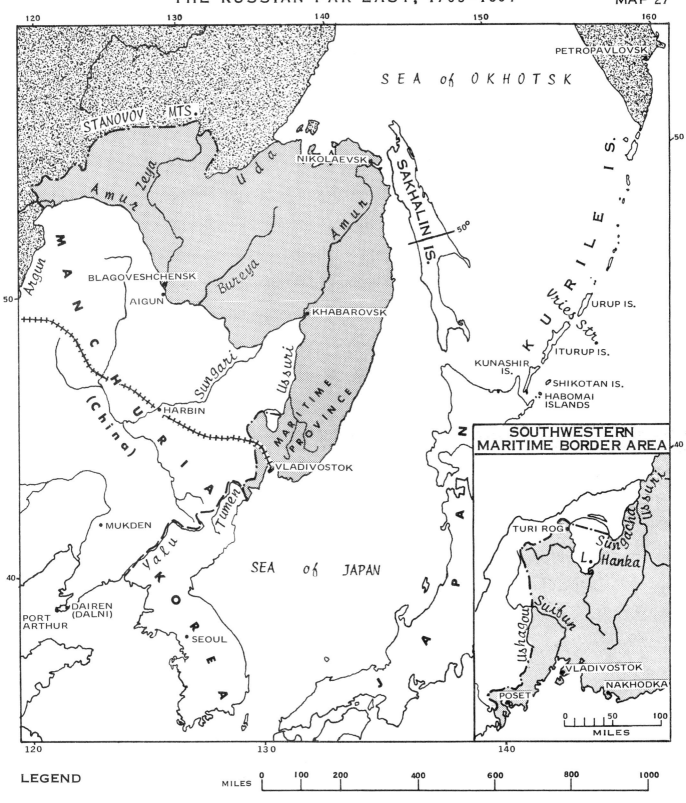

SEA of OKHOTSK

PETROPAVLOVSK

STANOVOY MTS.

NIKOLAEVSK

SAKHALIN IS.

KURILE IS.

URUP IS.

Vries Str.

ITURUP IS.

KUNASHIR IS.

SHIKOTAN IS.

HABOMAI ISLANDS

Amur

Zeya

Uda

Amur

Bureya

ARGUN

MANCHURIA (China)

BLAGOVESHCHENSK

AIGUN

KHABAROVSK

Sungari

HARBIN

Ussuri

MARITIME PROVINCE

VLADIVOSTOK

MUKDEN

Tumen

Valu

KOREA

SEA of JAPAN

PORT ARTHUR

DAIREN (DALNI)

SEOUL

J A P A N

SOUTHWESTERN MARITIME BORDER AREA

TURI ROG

Sungacha

Ussuri

L. Hanka

Ushagou

Suifun

VLADIVOSTOK

NAKHODKA

POSET

0   50   100
MILES

LEGEND

MILES   0   100   200   400   600   800   1000

RUSSIAN TERRITORY TO 1850 (NERCHINSK TREATY 1689)

AMUR AND MARITIME AREAS, ANNEXED 1858–60

KOREAN BORDER 1895 (SINO-JAPANESE PEACE TREATY)

++++++++++ PROJECTED ROUTE OF THE CHINESE EASTERN RAILROAD

the coast. Although the Chinese government refused to ratify the treaty, Russian encroachments continued: in July 1860 the port of Vladivostok was founded. China, reduced to impotence by the renewed attacks of the Western Powers, finally agreed to the Treaty of Peking in November 1860. By its terms, she ceded not only the left bank of the Amur, but also its right bank below the junction of the Ussuri, plus the right bank of the Ussuri itself (the Maritime province). In 1861, and again in 1886, Russo-Chinese commissions demarcated the Maritime borders (see insert, Map 27). The boundary ran, and still runs, along the Ussuri and Sunga-cha rivers to Lake Hanka (Khanka), the northern quarter of which is Manchurian, thence along ridge lines and part of the Ushagou (Wushe-kou) River, a southern tributary of the Suifun, to a point some ten miles north of the coast, where it follows the Tumen River (here separating Korea and Russia) to the sea.

The region of the confluence of the Amur and Ussuri rivers has been a source of friction. These rivers meet in two channels approximately 30 miles apart. The Russians claim that the border follows the western (Kazakevicheva) channel, and their control of the Hei-Hsia-Tzu Island lying between the two streams has been unsuccessfully contested.

Another seed of later dispute was the area along the left bank of the Amur between the Zeya and Bureya rivers. The Aigun Treaty of 1858 provided that the settlers in the "64 villages" of this region would remain under Manchu administration, but during the 1900 Boxer Rebellion the Russians expelled these inhabitants and assumed jurisdiction over the territory. This action has not been sanctioned by China.

Map 28. The Russian Far East, 1898–1945

The Russo-Japanese War of 1904–1905 and Its Aftermath

In 1898 Russia obtained a twenty-five-year lease on the southern tip of the Liaotung Peninsula, including Port Arthur and Dalni (Dairen), just three years after she had taken the diplomatic lead in forcing Japan to renounce her claim to that same Chinese area. Excluding Arctic islands, this was destined to be the last substantive addition to the Tsarist Empire. As noted above (page 86), in 1896 Russia had obtained extensive economic and administrative privileges in Manchuria along the right-of-way of the proposed Chinese Eastern Railroad (C.E.RR.), the shortcut between Vladivostok and the Trans-Siberian Railroad at Chita which was completed in 1903 (see insert, Map 28).

Along with the Liaotung concessions in 1898, Russia obtained the right to construct the Southern Manchurian Railroad, connecting Port Arthur with the C.E.RR. at Harbin. Russian influence was then felt throughout most of Manchuria. When Russia also extended her economic activities into Korea and refused Japanese offers for a division of spheres of influence, the Japanese struck the Russian fleet at Port Arthur in 1904, initiating a successful war against their imperialistic rival.

By the terms of the Portsmouth Peace Treaty in 1905, Russia ceded to Japan the southern half of Sakhalin Island (below 50° N. Latitude; see above, Map 27), the lease on the tip of the Liaotung Peninsula, and that portion of the Southern Manchurian Railroad from Changchun to Port Arthur. She also agreed to the mutual evacuation of Manchuria, which was to be restored to exclusive Chinese control.

However in 1911, taking advantage of the chaos accompanying the Chinese revolution and the collapse of the Ching Dynasty, Russia encroached about five miles into Manchuria along a sixty-mile front in the Manchouli region between Mongolia and the Argun River (see insert, Map 28). Neither the Republic of China nor the Communist regime has accepted the validity of the Tsitsihar Treaty which ceded this region of approximately 375 square miles; China claims that the agreement was

THE RUSSIAN FAR EAST, 1898–1945

MAP 28

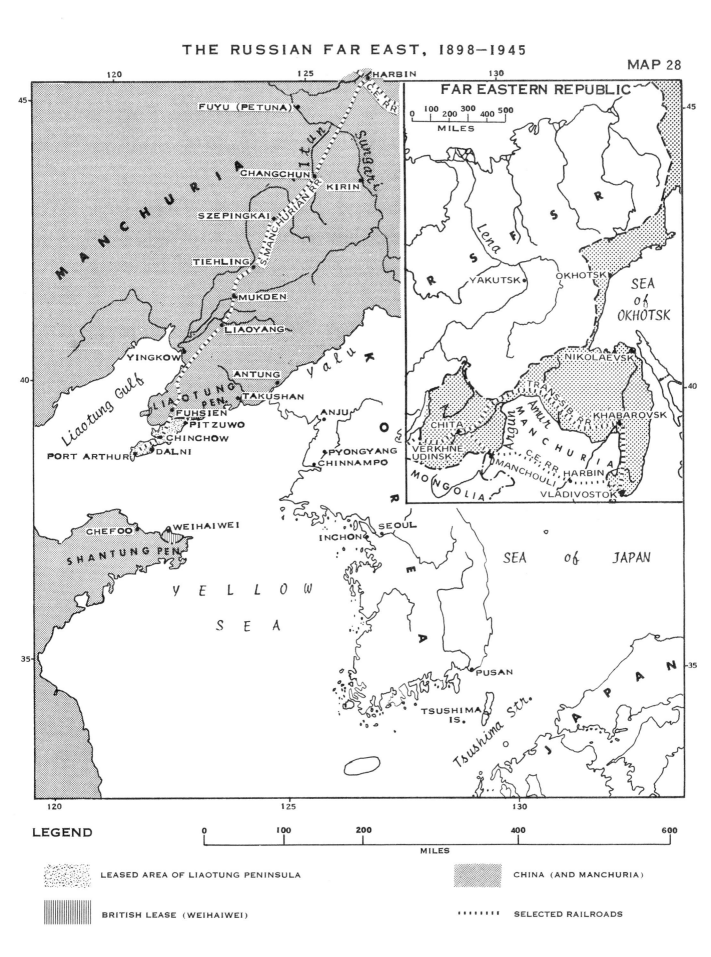

FAR EASTERN REPUBLIC

0 100 200 300 400 500
MILES

HARBIN
FUYU (PETUNA)
MANCHURIA
C.E.R.R.
Sungari
Itun
CHANGCHUN
KIRIN
S.MANCHURIAN RR.
SZEPINGKAI
TIEHLING
MUKDEN
LIAOYANG
YINGKOW
LIAOTUNG PEN.
ANTUNG
TAKUSHAN
FUHSIEN
PITZUWO
CHINCHOW
PORT ARTHUR
DALNI
Liaotung Gulf
Yalu
KOREA
ANJU
PYONGYANG
CHINNAMPO
CHEFOO
WEIHAIWEI
SHANTUNG PEN.
YELLOW SEA
SEOUL
INCHON
R.S.F.S.R.
Lena
YAKUTSK
OKHOTSK
SEA of OKHOTSK
NIKOLAEVSK
TRANS-SIB. RR.
Amur
MANCHURIA
KHABAROVSK
CHITA
Argun
VERKHNE UDINSK
C.E. RR.
HARBIN
MANCHOULI
MONGOLIA
VLADIVOSTOK
SEA of JAPAN
PUSAN
TSUSHIMA IS.
Tsushima Str.
JAPAN

LEGEND

0 100 200 400 600
MILES

LEASED AREA OF LIAOTUNG PENINSULA

CHINA (AND MANCHURIA)

BRITISH LEASE (WEIHAIWEI)

.... SELECTED RAILROADS

never ratified. This is but one more of many contested segments of the 4,150-mile-long Russo-Chinese frontier (approximately 2,300 miles of which lie east of Mongolia).

After this, Russia's borders in the Far East remained basically static until the end of the Second World War. The exceptions, not conceded by Russia, were those temporary alterations effected during the confused period of Allied intervention (1918–22), and the very minor changes related to border clashes with the Japanese during the late 1930s.

Seeing an opportunity for aggrandizement in the internal difficulties of Russia during the civil war period, Japan landed large forces in the Maritime province in 1918, seized the C.E.R.R., and occupied northern Sakhalin (1920). As a partial counter to Japanese designs, the Soviet regime fostered the Far Eastern Republic in 1920 (see insert, Map 28); shortly after Japanese forces withdrew from the mainland in 1922, the Republic was dissolved, and its territory incorporated into the Russian Soviet Federative Socialist Republic (R.S.F.S.R.). The Soviet government also regained partial control of the C.E.R.R. It sold its interest in the disputed railroad to the Japanese puppet state of Manchukuo in 1935.

In 1925 the Japanese finally signed a treaty with the Soviet government providing for the withdrawal of Japanese forces from northern Sakhalin in return for economic concessions. With this agreement, the territorial status quo as of 1905 was completely restored in the Russian Far East; it endured until the Second World War.

Map 29. The Brest-Litovsk Settlement, 1918

Initial Losses of Soviet Russia

A drastic contraction of Russia's western and southern frontiers was effected by the Treaty of Brest-Litovsk (3 March 1918), but this settlement lasted only eight months. A presumptuous Germany dictated a conqueror's peace, only to succumb herself to the Allied offensive in the fall of the same year.

By the terms of the treaty of 3 March, Russia was forced to renounce sovereignty over all territory lying west of an "agreed" line (see Map 29). This meant unconditional cession of Russian Poland, Lithuania, Kurland, and the cities of Vilna, Dvinsk, and Riga. Estonia and Livonia east of that line, which had already been seized by the German army, were to remain under German occupation pending the conclusion of "a general peace."

In a supplemental treaty, signed 27 August 1918, Russia also renounced sovereignty over Estonia and Livonia. Germany merely agreed to withdraw from the areas she had occupied east of those regions, including Pskov, after the demarcation of their eastern frontiers. At the same time, German evacuation of the territory east of the Berezina River was made dependent on the payment of reparations stipulated in a separate financial agreement of the same date.

The original Brest Treaty also required Russia to recognize the independence of the "Ukrainian People's Republic," which had signed a peace treaty with its German sponsor and her allies on 9 February 1918. In addition, the independence of Finland was reaffirmed (see below, page 96).

The treaty of 3 March also required Russia to withdraw her forces from the areas in Eastern Anatolia captured from Turkey and to retrocede the districts of Kars, Ardahan, and Batumi, which she had annexed in 1878.

Vast as these Russian cessions were, the areas actually held by the German army and its allies were even greater. In the spring and summer

92

THE BREST–LITOVSK SETTLEMENT, 1918

MAP 29

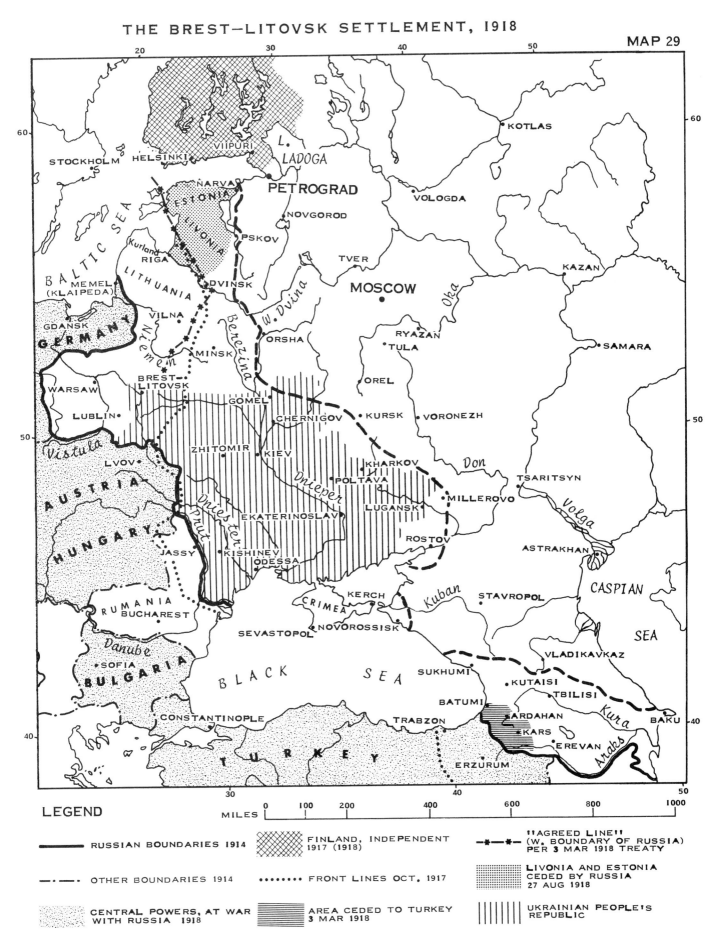

LEGEND   MILES

| 0 | 100 | 200 | 400 | 600 | 800 | 1000 |

—————— RUSSIAN BOUNDARIES 1914

FINLAND, INDEPENDENT 1917 (1918)

—x—x— "AGREED LINE" (W. BOUNDARY OF RUSSIA) PER 3 MAR 1918 TREATY

—·—·— OTHER BOUNDARIES 1914

········· FRONT LINES OCT, 1917

LIVONIA AND ESTONIA CEDED BY RUSSIA 27 AUG 1918

CENTRAL POWERS, AT WAR WITH RUSSIA 1918

AREA CEDED TO TURKEY 3 MAR 1918

UKRAINIAN PEOPLE'S REPUBLIC

— — — FARTHEST ADVANCES OF CENTRAL POWERS 1918

of 1918 they occupied not only the Ukraine but also the lower Don basin, the Crimea, the lower Kuban River region, including the port of Novo-rossisk, and most of the Caucasus, including the vital Baku oilfields. In the treaty of 27 August, Germany conditionally promised to evacuate the Black Sea territory outside the Caucasus, while Russia agreed to German recognition of the independence of Georgia. However, it was not these German promises but defeat in the west which led to the eventual withdrawal of the German armies from Russia.

Both the March and August treaties were abrogated when the German Empire collapsed in November 1918. The Council of People's Commissars decreed the annulment of the Brest Treaty on 9 November, and four days later the Central Executive Committee of the Soviets made this formal. The Allied–German Armistice agreement of 11 November also proclaimed the annulment of the Brest-Litovsk "and supplemental treaties," and the Versailles Treaty reiterated Germany's renunciation of the treaty.

Russia had been saved from the dire consequences of Brest-Litovsk by unpredictable circumstances. However, some of the losses were permanent (see below, pages 96–98).

Map 30. European Russia, 1918–1938

Russian Losses in the West, 1918–1921

Most of the western territories annexed by Peter I, Catherine II, and Alexander I were lost to Russia within a year of the fall of the Tsarist Empire. After the abrogation of the Brest-Litovsk Treaty in November 1918, these areas either achieved or reaffirmed their independence.

Finland's independence, announced in December 1917, was officially recognized by the Soviet government on 4 January 1918. The Brest-Litovsk agreement also provided for the withdrawal of Russian troops from Finland and the Aaland Islands. After the civil war in Finland and the skirmishing in Eastern Karelia had terminated, the Russian Soviet Federative Socialist Republic (R.S.F.S.R.) and the new Finnish Republic concluded the formal Peace of Tartu on 14 October 1920. Finland's boundaries were essentially those of the Duchy after 1833; she retained Vyborg and the Karelian Isthmus to a point about twenty miles from Petrograd, renamed Leningrad in 1924. The treaty also transferred the Petsamo (Pechenga) region and the western end of the Rybachi (Fisher) and Sredni peninsulas to Finland, giving her an outlet on the Barents Sea. The western part of these peninsulas was returned to Russia in 1940, and the Pechenga area was retroceded in 1944, formally in 1947 (see below, Map 31 insert and Map 32).

The Baltic states of Lithuania and Estonia both declared their independence in February 1918, and Latvia followed suit in November. Russia was forced to yield the Lithuanian area by the Brest-Litovsk Treaty, and she renounced her claim to the Estonian and Latvian regions by the supplementary treaty of August 1918 (see above, page 92). The R.S.F.S.R. concluded formal peace treaties with these new states in 1920: with Estonia 2 February, Lithuania 12 July, and Latvia 11 August. In the last case, the Russian border was moved east of the border established by the Brest-Litovsk settlement; the independent state of Latvia included the province of Latgale in the southeast (compare Maps 29 and 30).

Poland, which had also declared its independence in 1918, launched

96

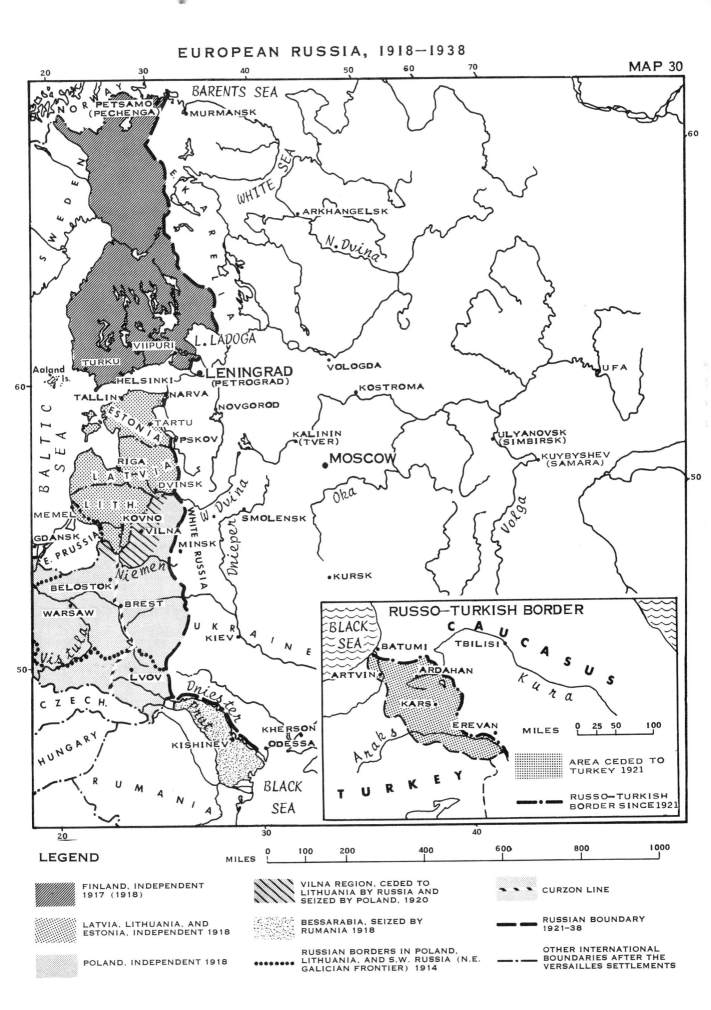

EUROPEAN RUSSIA, 1918–1938

BARENTS SEA

PETSAMO (PECHENGA)

MURMANSK

NORWAY

SWEDEN

E. KARELIA

WHITE SEA

ARKHANGELSK

N. Dvina

VIIPURI

L. LADOGA

TURKU

HELSINKI

Aaland Is.

LENINGRAD (PETROGRAD)

VOLOGDA

UFA

TALLIN

NARVA

ESTONIA

TARTU

PSKOV

NOVGOROD

KALININ (TVER)

KOSTROMA

ULYANOVSK (SIMBIRSK)

BALTIC SEA

RIGA

LATVIA

DVINSK

LITH.

MEMEL

KOVNO

VILNA

GDANSK

E. PRUSSIA

Niemen

MINSK

W. Dvina

WHITE RUSSIA

MOSCOW

Oka

KUYBYSHEV (SAMARA)

SMOLENSK

Dnieper

Volga

BELOSTOK

BREST

WARSAW

Vistula

UKRAINE

KIEV

KURSK

LVOV

Dniester

Prut

KISHINEV

KHERSON

ODESSA

CZECH.

HUNGARY

RUMANIA

BLACK SEA

RUSSO–TURKISH BORDER

BLACK SEA

CAUCASUS

BATUMI

TBILISI

ARTVIN

ARDAHAN

Kura

KARS

Araks

EREVAN

MILES   0 25 50 100

TURKEY

AREA CEDED TO TURKEY 1921

RUSSO–TURKISH BORDER SINCE 1921

MILES   0 100 200 400 600 800 1000

LEGEND

FINLAND, INDEPENDENT 1917 (1918)

VILNA REGION, CEDED TO LITHUANIA BY RUSSIA AND SEIZED BY POLAND, 1920

CURZON LINE

LATVIA, LITHUANIA, AND ESTONIA, INDEPENDENT 1918

BESSARABIA, SEIZED BY RUMANIA 1918

RUSSIAN BOUNDARY 1921–38

POLAND, INDEPENDENT 1918

RUSSIAN BORDERS IN POLAND, LITHUANIA, AND S.W. RUSSIA (N.E. GALICIAN FRONTIER) 1914

OTHER INTERNATIONAL BOUNDARIES AFTER THE VERSAILLES SETTLEMENTS an offensive against Russia in 1920 to conquer the Ukraine. The seesaw campaigns resulted in the compromise Peace of Riga on 18 March 1921. Poland's boundary, which was considerably east of the Curzon Line proposed by the Allies, included parts of White Russia and the Ukraine, as well as the Vilna area which Russia had ceded to Lithuania in 1920. The new Polish nation was much larger than Congress Poland, but not as large as the Poland of 1772.

Rumania also took advantage of the turmoil in Russia to seize Bessarabia in January 1918. Unlike the other border changes mentioned here, the loss of this region was never formally recognized by the Soviet government. (For a detailed map of Bessarabia, see above, Map 23.)

Finally, as noted above (page 92), Russia lost Batumi, Kars, and Ardahan to the Turks in 1918. By the terms of the treaty signed in 1921, Russia regained the important oil port of Batumi, but the latter two areas remained Turkish (see insert, Map 30). Their common boundary, which has not changed since 1921, is approximately 335 miles long.

There were numerous other temporary boundary changes during the period of the civil war and the intervention in Russia, including Georgia's severance from Russia for a three-year period beginning in 1918, but those mentioned above were the only ones of any duration. By 1921 Russia's western frontiers had been stabilized; they remained so until 1939.

Map 31. European Russia, 1939–1941

The Period of Nazi–Soviet Collaboration

Soon after the signing of the Hitler–Stalin treaty (23 August 1939), Soviet Russia began implementing her part of the division of Eastern Europe which it outlined.

On 17 September Russian forces invaded Poland, already tottering under the German onslaught, and organized resistance was quickly crushed. On 28 September a new treaty was signed which established the Russo-German boundary partially along the middle of the Western Bug River, rather than along the Vistula which had been agreed upon in August; in exchange, the Soviet sphere of influence was extended to most of Lithuania. This fourth partition restored to Russia essentially the same Polish borderlands as the third partition (1795), plus eastern Galicia.

The next additions to Soviet territory were made at Finland's expense, after a brief but costly war. The peace treaty, ratified on 20 March 1940, gave the U.S.S.R. the strategic Karelian Isthmus, including Vyborg (Viipuri), several tiny islands in the Gulf of Finland, the western and northwestern shores of Lake Ladoga, the Finnish part of the Rybachi and Sredni peninsulas (see insert, Map 31), the Arctic Circle region surrounding Salla (renamed Kuolayarvi by the Russians in 1940, the same year that the Finns renamed the village of Kursu, thirty miles west, their new Salla), and a thirty-year lease on Hanko Cape. Among the islands ceded to Russia were Tyutyarsari, Lavansaari, Seyskari, and Sur-Sari. Although they are too small to depict in detail at the scale of these maps, they are strategically located on the approach to Leningrad, lying at approximately 60° N. Latitude between 27° and 28°30′ E. Longitude.

In June 1940 a Soviet ultimatum forced Rumania to cede Bessarabia and Northern Bukovina, including the former capital city of Chernovtsy. Russia also seized the town of Gertsa (Herta) and approximately 150 square miles of surrounding territory in Moldavia. In August the Moldavian S.S.R. was established, combining the former Autonomous S.S.R.

100

EUROPEAN RUSSIA, 1939-1941

MAP 31

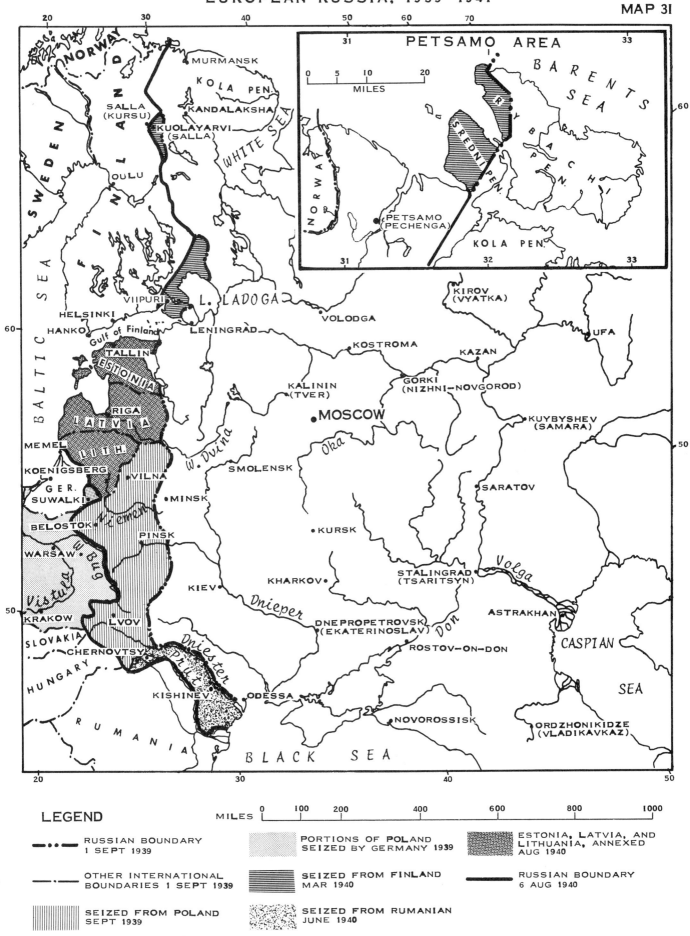

PETSAMO AREA

BARENTS SEA

NORWAY

SREDNI PEN.

RYBACHI PEN.

PETSAMO (PECHENGA)

KOLA PEN.

MILES
0 5 10 20

NORWAY

MURMANSK

KOLA PEN.

KANDALAKSHA

SALLA (KURSU)

KUOLAYARVI (SALLA)

WHITE SEA

SWEDEN

FINLAND

OULU

VIIPURI

L. LADOGA

KIROV (VYATKA)

VOLODGA

UFA

HELSINKI

HANKO

Gulf of Finland

LENINGRAD

KOSTROMA

KAZAN

BALTIC SEA

TALLIN

ESTONIA

RIGA

LATVIA

KALININ (TVER)

GORKI (NIZHNI-NOVGOROD)

MOSCOW

KUYBYSHEV (SAMARA)

MEMEL

LITH.

KOENIGSBERG

VILNA

W. Dvina

SMOLENSK

Oka

SARATOV

GER. SUWALKI

Niemen

MINSK

KURSK

BELOSTOK

PINSK

WARSAW

W. Bug

KIEV

KHARKOV

STALINGRAD (TSARITSYN)

Volga

Vistula

KRAKOW

LVOV

Dnieper

DNEPROPETROVSK (EKATERINOSLAV)

Don

ASTRAKHAN

SLOVAKIA

CHERNOVTSY

Dniester

ROSTOV-ON-DON

CASPIAN SEA

HUNGARY

Prut

KISHINEV

ODESSA

RUMANIA

NOVOROSSISK

ORDZHONIKIDZE (VLADIKAVKAZ)

BLACK SEA

LEGEND

MILES
0 100 200 400 600 800 1000

— ·· — ·· — **RUSSIAN BOUNDARY 1 SEPT 1939**

— · — **OTHER INTERNATIONAL BOUNDARIES 1 SEPT 1939**

SEIZED FROM POLAND SEPT 1939

PORTIONS OF POLAND SEIZED BY GERMANY 1939

SEIZED FROM FINLAND MAR 1940

SEIZED FROM RUMANIAN JUNE 1940

ESTONIA, LATVIA, AND LITHUANIA, ANNEXED AUG 1940

RUSSIAN BOUNDARY 6 AUG 1940

with the predominantly Rumanian-speaking portions of Bessarabia. Northern Bukovina and the Gertsa region, which had never been part of the Russian Empire, and the predominantly Ukrainian-speaking districts of Bessarabia were then incorporated into the Ukrainian S.S.R. (For a more detailed view of these areas, see above, Map 23. The annexed portion of Bukovina lies mainly between the Suceava and Cheremosh rivers, extending north to the upper Dniester.)

The final acquisitions of this period were the Baltic states of Lithuania, Latvia, and Estonia, formally annexed on 3, 5, and 6 August 1940, respectively. Soviet forces had garrisoned these defenseless nations since the fall of 1939, and in July 1940 they were organized as Soviet Socialist Republics. All that remained to be done in August was to perform the ceremony of their "voluntary" reunion with Russia. Incidentally, when Russian forces took over Lithuania, they also occupied the southwestern portion which fell within the German sphere of influence as specified by the agreement of 28 September 1939.

Map 32. Russian Acquisitions, 1944–1956

Russian Expansion Resulting from World War II

As she always did after a successful war, Russia expanded her borders following the defeat of Nazi Germany and Japan.

In 1944 the Russian army occupied the Pechenga (Petsamo) region, cutting off Finland's outlet to the Arctic Ocean. The peace treaty of 1947 confirmed the annexation of this region to the R.S.F.S.R., giving the Soviet Union about 122 miles of common frontier with Norway (see Map 32 and insert, Map 31). This new boundary is the same as the pre-1917 border in the Petsamo region, with the exception of a small area around the Jäniskoski hydroelectric power station on the Pasvik (Pats) River, which the U.S.S.R. acquired one week before the 1947 peace treaty was signed. With that peace settlement the Russian lease on Hanko, secured in 1940, was exchanged for a fifty-year lease on a naval base in the Porkkala region, only twelve miles from Helsinki; the latter area was returned to Finland in 1955. The other regions ceded to the Finns in 1940 (see above, page 100) were also confirmed as Russian by the 1947 treaty. Since these changes, only 313 miles of the approximately 822 miles of Soviet-Finnish border remain the same as the 1920 boundary.

The Soviet annexation of the northern part of East Prussia, including Koenigsberg (renamed Kaliningrad in 1946), was an unprecedented extension of Russia's western frontier. The importance attached to this strategic Baltic outpost was emphasized by its incorporation into the R.S.F.S.R., rather than into the contiguous Lithuanian S.S.R.

The Lithuanian S.S.R. acquired the bordering Memel (Klaipeda) Territory from Germany in 1945. This narrow strip along the right bank of the lower Niemen River and the Baltic coast had been under Lithuanian control from 1923 to March 1939, when it had been returned to Germany.

104

RUSSIAN ACQUISITIONS, 1944–1956

MAP 32

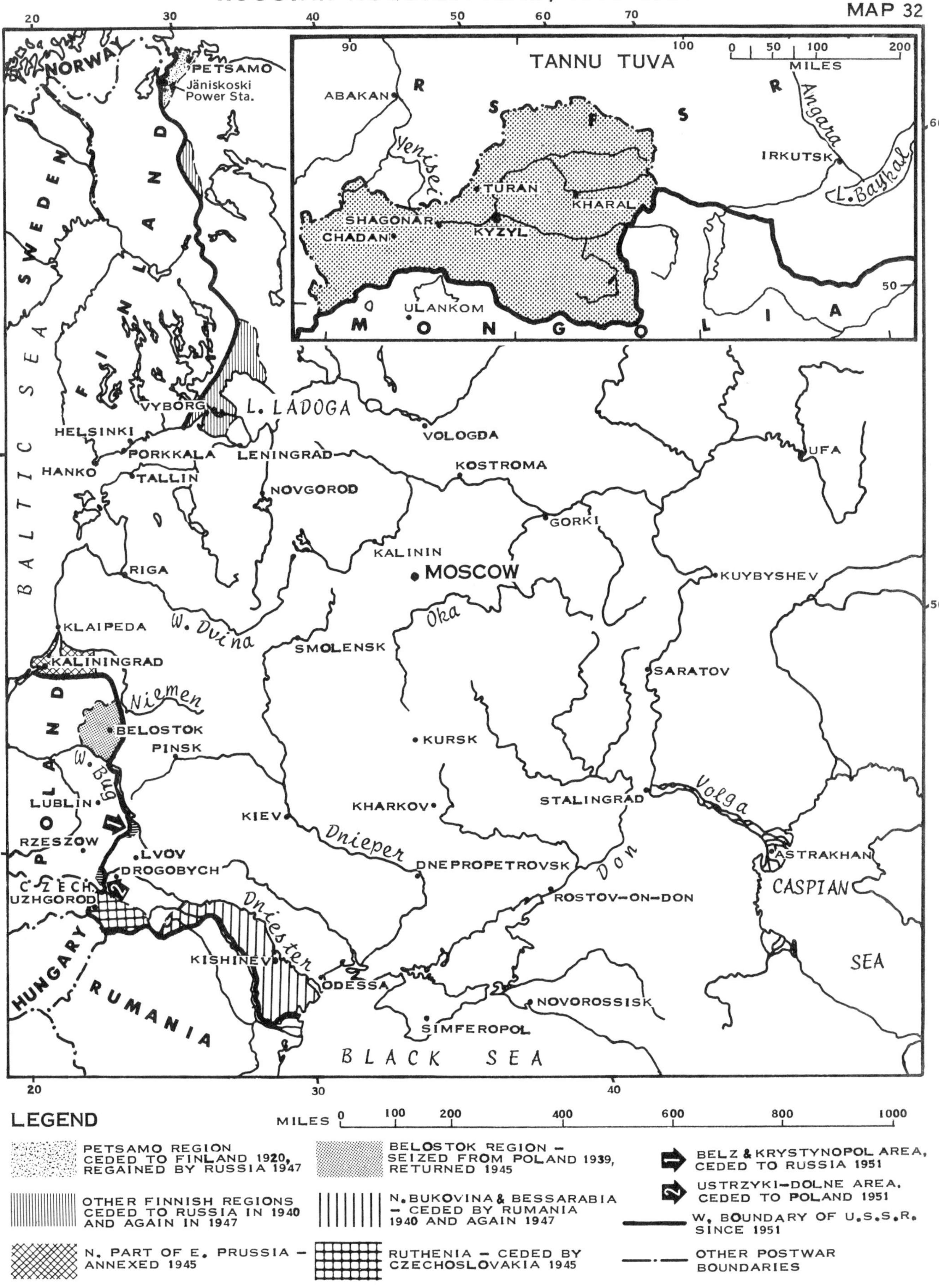

TANNU TUVA
MILES
0 50 100 200
R S F S R
Angara
ABAKAN
Yenisei
IRKUTSK
L. Baykal
TURAN
KHARAL
SHAGONAR
KYZYL
CHADAN
ULANKOM
M O N G O L I A
NORWAY
PETSAMO
Jäniskoski Power Sta.
SWEDEN
FINLAND
BALTIC SEA
VYBORG
L. LADOGA
HELSINKI
PORKKALA
HANKO
TALLIN
LENINGRAD
VOLOGDA
KOSTROMA
NOVGOROD
GORKI
UFA
KALININ
MOSCOW
KUYBYSHEV
RIGA
W. Dvina
Oka
KLAIPEDA
SMOLENSK
KALININGRAD
SARATOV
Niemen
POLAND
BELOSTOK
PINSK
KURSK
W. Bug
LUBLIN
KHARKOV
STALINGRAD
Volga
KIEV
Dnieper
RZESZOW
LVOV
ASTRAKHAN
DNEPROPETROVSK
Don
CZECH.
DROGOBYCH
UZHGOROD
CASPIAN SEA
ROSTOV-ON-DON
Dniester
HUNGARY
KISHINEV
ODESSA
RUMANIA
NOVOROSSISK
SIMFEROPOL
BLACK SEA
LEGEND
MILES 0 100 200 400 600 800 1000
PETSAMO REGION CEDED TO FINLAND 1920, REGAINED BY RUSSIA 1947
BELOSTOK REGION – SEIZED FROM POLAND 1939, RETURNED 1945
BELZ & KRYSTYNOPOL AREA, CEDED TO RUSSIA 1951
OTHER FINNISH REGIONS CEDED TO RUSSIA IN 1940 AND AGAIN IN 1947
N. BUKOVINA & BESSARABIA – CEDED BY RUMANIA 1940 AND AGAIN 1947
USTRZYKI-DOLNE AREA, CEDED TO POLAND 1951
W. BOUNDARY OF U.S.S.R. SINCE 1951
N. PART OF E. PRUSSIA – ANNEXED 1945
RUTHENIA – CEDED BY CZECHOSLOVAKIA 1945
OTHER POSTWAR BOUNDARIES

Poland was forced to accept compensation in the west (as well as in southern East Prussia) for her losses in the east. Her postwar border with the U.S.S.R. is generally the same as the Russo-German line of September 1939. An exception is the Belostok Oblast (region), which Russia returned to Poland under the terms of the frontier treaty of 16 August 1945. In February 1951 a minor exchange of territories was effected (approximately 185 square miles in each case): the area around Belz and Krystynopol, part of Poland's Lublin province, was annexed to the Ukrainian S.S.R.; and the Russian-held Ustrzyki-Dolne area of the Drogobych region was attached to Poland's Rzeszow province.

Czechoslovakia also lost territory to Russia: Ruthenia, also known as Transcarpathian Ukraine, was formally ceded to the Soviet Union by the Treaty of 29 June 1945, when it was incorporated into the Ukrainian S.S.R. as the Transcarpathian Oblast. The province, with its capital of Uzhgorod, had been seized by Hungary in 1939 and conquered by Russian forces in 1944; it had never been part of the Russian Empire. As a result of this annexation, the Soviet Union borders Czechoslovakia for approximately 60 miles and Hungary for about 75 miles.

The 1947 peace treaty between the U.S.S.R. and Rumania confirmed the Russian annexation of Bessarabia, Northern Bukovina, and the Gertsa region which had initially been effected in 1940 (see above, pages 100–02). Rumania now shares approximately 839 miles of frontier with the Soviet Union.

In the east, an incidental result of the war was the incorporation of the Tannu Tuva area into the R.S.F.S.R. in 1944 as the Tuvinian Autonomous Oblast (see insert, Map 32). This sparsely populated northwestern corner of Outer Mongolia had been a Russian protectorate from 1914 to 1921 and a nominally independent People's Republic from 1921 to 1944.

The defeat of Japan resulted in Soviet occupation and annexation of Southern Sakhalin, Japanese since 1905, and the Kurile Islands, Japanese since 1855–75 (see above, page 84). Their reannexation by Russia was agreed upon at Yalta in 1945, and both areas were incorporated into the Sakhalin Oblast of the R.S.F.S.R. later that year. To date there has not been a final peace treaty between Japan and the Soviet Union; in October 1956 these nations issued a joint "declaration," in which Russia agreed to return the Habomai and Shikotan islands to Japan "after the conclusion of a peace treaty" (see above, Map 27). Since these small islands (which lie south of Kunashir Island, the nearest to Japan of the large Kurile Islands) were the only ones mentioned in the declaration, it might appear that Japan recognized Soviet control of the major islands by default. However, continuing Japanese interest in Kunashir and Iturup (Japanese Etorofu) islands remains an obstacle to a formal peace treaty.

Russia also profited at China's expense in 1945, but these gains lasted only a decade or less. They included reassertion of Russian interest in, and virtual control of, the Chinese Eastern and Southern Manchurian railroads, and joint control, with China, of the port of Dairen and the Port Arthur naval base (see above, Map 28). By 1955 Russia had yielded all of these gains to her new "ally," Communist China.

Map 33. Russia's Arctic Islands, Fifteenth–Twentieth Centuries

Strategic Outposts on the Polar Air Route

It is impractical to discuss here all of the small islands off the thousands of miles of Russia's Arctic coast. However, there are a few large islands and archipelagoes which have assumed strategic significance in this air age. The conflicting historic claims to certain of these areas, and the obscurity concerning their discovery, are not as important as the fact of their present possession by the U.S.S.R.

The two large islands known together as Novaya Zemlya (New Land), which are separated by the very narrow Matochkin Shar Strait, were, on account of their proximity to European Russia, the first of these Arctic regions visited by Russians. There were occasional voyages to the islands in the fifteenth century, and more frequent ones in the sixteenth. They came to be considered Russian territory during the 1500s, although they were not systematically explored until the nineteenth century. They are currently under the jurisdiction of the R.S.F.S.R., as are all of the other islands discussed below.

Chronologically, the next Arctic islands discovered by Russians were the Novosibirskie (New Siberian) Islands, a large archipelago extending from approximately 73°–77° N. Latitude and 133°–158°30′ E. Longitude. First visited early in the eighteenth century, they were rediscovered and claimed by Russia about 1773.

Severnaya Zemlya (Northern Land), which comprises four large and numerous small islands, was discovered and claimed in 1913. Extending from approximately 77°50′–81°15′ N. Latitude and 90°–107°50′ E. Longitude, the islands were thoroughly explored by a Soviet expedition in the early 1930s.

Wrangel Island, which lies off northeastern Siberia at 71° N. Latitude, 180° Longitude, may possibly have been visited by a Russian navigator in the eighteenth century, although it was not explored until 1911.

108

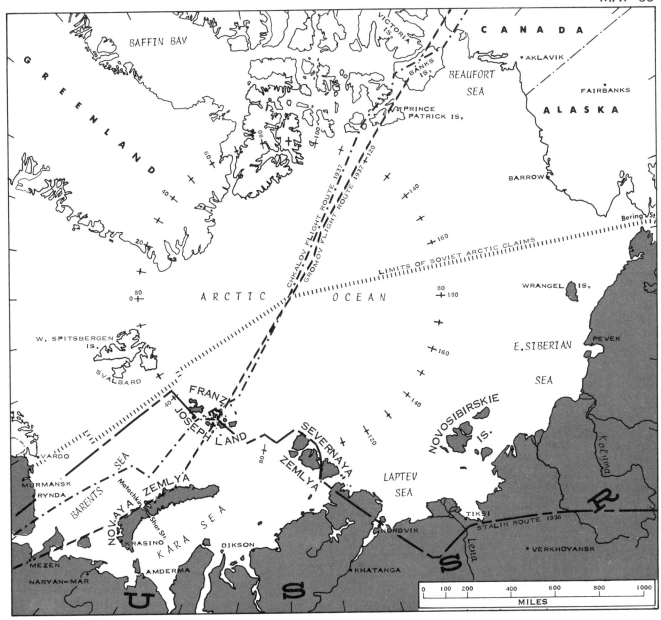

The Tsarist government advanced its claim to the island in 1916, but this was disputed in the 1920s. In 1926 the Soviet government included Wrangel Island in a general claim to the islands off its Arctic coast, and a Soviet station was established there in the same year.

The last of these regions to be explored and claimed by Russia was Franz Joseph Land, an archipelago of numerous isles lying between 42°10′–65° E. Longitude and 79°45′–81°50′ N. Latitude, the most northerly land in the Eastern Hemisphere. Although discovered by an Austro-Hungarian expedition in 1873, and named for their emperor, these islands were visited by Russian expeditions in the second decade of the twentieth century and formally claimed by the U.S.S.R. in 1926.

Some of the pioneer air routes over these islands are illustrated on the accompanying map. The first Arctic seaplane flights were made in 1914 from Novaya Zemlya. The nonstop Arctic flight along the "Stalin Route," undertaken in 1936, crossed both Franz Joseph Land and Severnaya Zemlya. The famous Chkalov flight from Moscow to Vancouver, Washington, in June of 1937—the first trans-Polar airplane flight— passed over Franz Joseph Land. The record-breaking long-distance flight of Gromov the next month (Moscow–San Jacinto, California) crossed both Novaya Zemlya and Franz Joseph Land en route to the Pole. While those flights were widely publicized, the Soviet government has been more reticent about later Arctic airway developments.

The military potential of these Soviet islands, in conjunction with the numerous mainland Arctic bases, becomes obvious when the distances to North America via the Polar route are considered. For example, the distance from Murmansk to Washington, D.C., is only about 4,200 miles; from Igarka (above the Arctic Circle on the Yenisei River) to Seattle, Washington, is less than 4,500 miles. From bases on the island outposts, even these relatively short distances can be reduced by several hundred miles.

Map 34. Contemporary U.S.S.R.

Russia Today

The U.S.S.R. presently comprises an area, including the surface of closed bays, of approximately 8,600,000 square miles, or about one-sixth of the earth's inhabited surface. It is nearly three times as large as continental United States. Measured from its most distant points, it stretches approximately 7,000 miles east to west and 3,000 miles north to south. It has the longest coastline in the world, though much of this area is frozen wasteland. Its current borders total more than 35,000 miles: there have been only minor frontier adjustments since the settlements related to the Second World War, although there have been numerous internal administrative boundary changes.

Despite Soviet expansion, the U.S.S.R. today is approximately the same size as the Russian Empire of 1914. The cession of Finland in 1917 was only partially offset, in terms of territory, by the numerous but minor additions of 1939 and 1940. Even with postwar annexations included, the Soviet Union is only about 39,000 square miles larger than Tsarist Russia. However, there are now approximately 83 million more inhabitants (the comparison is for the area encompassed by the present frontiers); Soviet estimates for 1970 and 1913 are 242 million and 159 million, respectively.

As presently constituted, there are fifteen Union Republics in the U.S.S.R. By far the largest is the Russian Soviet Federative Socialist Republic (R.S.F.S.R.), which—because it is controlled directly from Moscow—comprises many of the most strategic areas, such as the Kaliningrad region and the Arctic islands.

The other Union Republics, or Soviet Socialist Republics (S.S.R.'s), in descending order of size, are: the Kazakh, Ukrainian (the largest in population, after the R.S.F.S.R.), Turkmen, Uzbek, Belorussian, Kirgiz, Tadzhik, Azerbaidzhan, Georgian, Lithuanian, Latvian, Estonian, Moldavian, and Armenian. This enumeration is in itself a review of much of Russia's history. Like its Tsarist predecessor, the Soviet Union remains a vast and heterogeneous empire.

KALININGRAD

BALTIC SEA

2
3 RIGA 1 TALLIN
VILNA
LENINGRÁD
MINSK PETROZAVODSK
MURMANSK
ARKHÁNGELSK
LVOV 4
Dnieper
UKRAIN KIEV
SSR
IAN YAROSLAVL
N. Dvina
Ob
NORILSK
5
KISHINEV
ODESSA TULA MOSCOW
KHARKOV GORKI
DNEPROPETROVSK
ZAPOROZHE KAZAN
R
DONETSK PERM
ROSTOV Volga NIZHNI-TAGIL
Don KUYBYSHEV SVERDLOVSK S
VOLGOGRAD UFA
(STALINGRAD)
ORENBURG CHELYABINSK Irtysh
MAGNITOGORSK
BATUMI ASTRAKHAN K OMSK Ob KRASNOYAR
6 A NOVOSIBIRSK
TBILISI Z
7 A TSELINOGRAD BARNAUL NOVO-
EREVAN KUZNETSK
8 8 KARAGANDA K
BAKU SEMIPALATINSK H
CASPIAN SEA ARAL
SEA Syr-Darya
U
Z
TURKMEN B
E
ASHKHABAD K Amu-Darya TASHKENT
BUKHARA ALMA-ATA
SSR S FRUNZE
S KIRGIZ
R DUSHANBE SSR
TADZHIK
SSR

BLACK SEA

Prut

W.Bug

Arabs

SOVIET ARCTIC CLAIMS

60

20

40

40

40

60 80

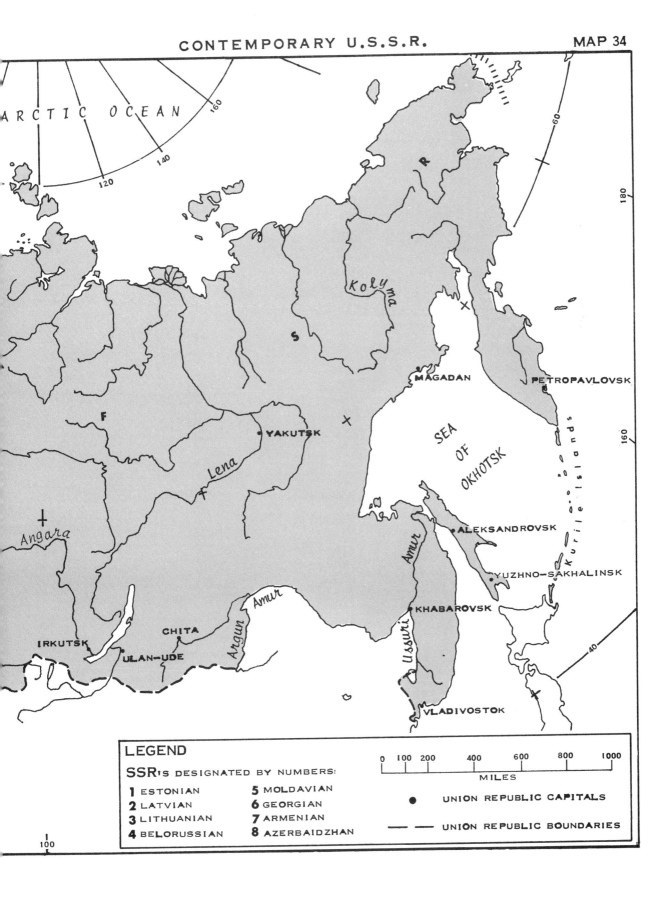

ARCTIC OCEAN

Kolyma

R

S

F

MAGADAN   PETROPAVLOVSK

YAKUTSK

Lena

SEA OF OKHOTSK

Kurile Islands

Angara

ALEKSANDROVSK

YUZHNO-SAKHALINSK

Amur

KHABAROVSK

Argun   Amur

CHITA

Ussuri

IRKUTSK

ULAN-UDE

VLADIVOSTOK

LEGEND

SSRs DESIGNATED BY NUMBERS:

1 ESTONIAN   5 MOLDAVIAN
2 LATVIAN   6 GEORGIAN
3 LITHUANIAN   7 ARMENIAN
4 BELORUSSIAN   8 AZERBAIDZHAN

0 100 200 400 600 800 1000
MILES

● UNION REPUBLIC CAPITALS

--- UNION REPUBLIC BOUNDARIES

Map 35. Vegetation Zones

Maps 36A and 36B. Temperature and Precipitation

Vegetation and Climate as Factors in Russia's History

The role of rivers in the consolidation and expansion of the Russian state has been noted above (Maps 1, 7, and 16). Other geographic factors are also pertinent to an understanding of its historical development.

Flying due north from Astrakhan on the Caspian Sea to the Arctic coast, one may view at least five different landscapes (as classified below), whereas one could fly eastward from the Baltic Sea across the entire length of the U.S.S.R. at 60° N. Latitude with scarcely a break in the monotonous taiga scenery. Major vegetation zones commonly stretch east and west across the vast Soviet Eurasian land mass.

More than 1.25 million square miles of inhospitable tundra encompass the entire Arctic coast, except for the completely barren wasteland south of Severnaya Zemlya (see Map 35). East of the Kola Peninsula (where the moderating influence of the Gulf Stream ends), the tundra generally extends to the Arctic Circle; exceptions like the Lena Valley are more than compensated for in the extreme northeast, where tundra stretches south of 60° N. in highland areas. It generally coincides with regions of permafrost, although the latter phenomenon is much more extensive, extending south of 55° N. just east of Lake Baykal, with patches of this permanently frozen subsoil as far south as the Soviet-Mongolian border. The areas shown on Map 36B with an average temperature less than 14° F. for more than 150 days a year roughly correspond to the permafrost regions.

As millions of square miles are too cold for farming, the desolate north is very sparsely inhabited. Most settlements are located where valuable natural resources justify the expense of importing the necessities of life. Access to these remote areas has been facilitated in recent decades by the development of air transport and technical improvements in operations on the seasonally navigable Northern Sea Route.

114

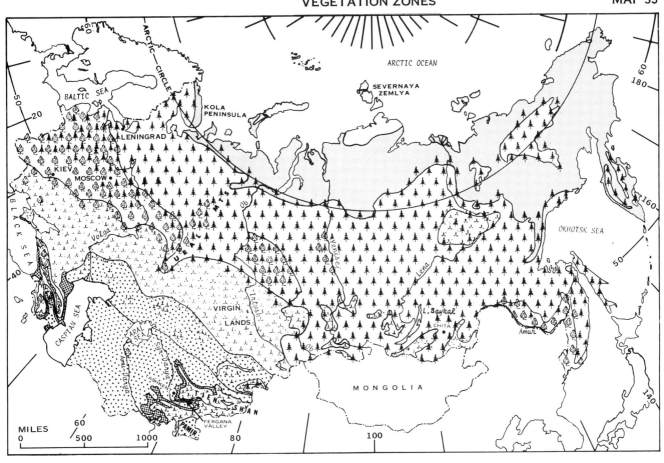

LEGEND

☐ ARCTIC WASTE		▥ MIXED FOREST		▦ DESERT	
▨ TUNDRA		▥ STEPPE		▦ SUBTROPICAL	
♠ TAIGA		▦ SEMI-DESERT		▦ ALPINE MEADOWS	

South of the tundra lie some 4 million square miles of taiga, the world's largest coniferous forest. As where other regions meet, there is a transition zone here—in this case wooded tundra and taiga interspersed with tundra. Most of the Siberian taiga is snow-covered for half the year or longer (see Map 36B).

For centuries, the products of Russia's limitless forests have been important to both her domestic economy and foreign trade. Furs were the magnet that drew the traders of medieval Novgorod as far as the Urals (see Map 4), and the same attraction sparked the conquest of Siberia (see Map 16). In more recent times, timber and wood products have been a major Russian export.

Even today, the vast majority of the taiga land east of the Urals has less than one inhabitant per square kilometer (less than 2.6 per square mile). Along the great river valleys, which remain the only north and south routes through most of this primordial forest, the average density is only 2.6 to 26 per square mile. Chita, situated on the Trans-Siberian Railroad, is one of the very few major cities in the Siberian taiga proper.

Below the taiga in Europe, and in a narrow belt in the Far East, are mixed and deciduous woods. Both Kiev and Moscow, centers of Russia's main historical development, lie in this forest zone.

Long before the formation of Kievan Rus, Eastern Slavs inhabited river valleys of these European woods. They gradually expanded deeper into the wild forests to the north and northeast, slowed more by the region's severe nature than by the weak Lithuanian and Finnish tribes they encountered.

Crops were grown on fields burned out of the woods, but both climate and soil limited farming in most of the mixed forest zone. Surplus population was supported by handicrafts and commerce along the plentiful rivers.

As noted above (Map 7), the deep protective woods surrounding Moscow were a factor in its growth at a time when older cities in the southeast were declining because of their exposure to attacks from the steppes. Both Kievan Rus and Muscovy were plagued for centuries by nomadic steppe tribes.

The steppe zone, wooded in patches along its northern fringe but predominately open grassland, served in early times as an unrestricted

116

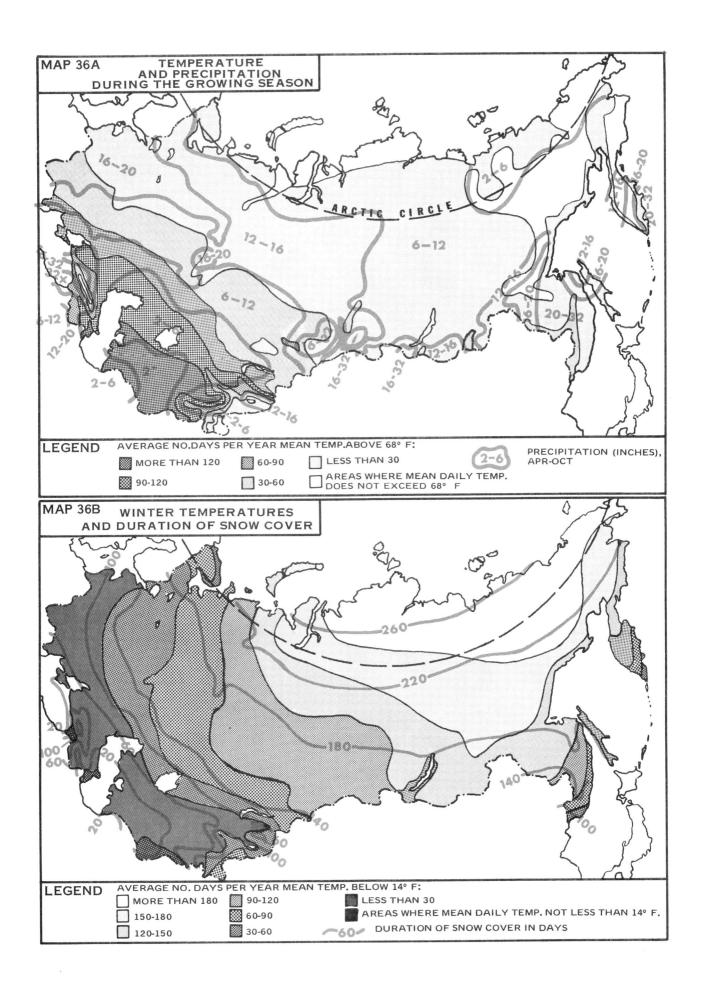

MAP 36A — TEMPERATURE AND PRECIPITATION DURING THE GROWING SEASON

ARCTIC CIRCLE

LEGEND   AVERAGE NO. DAYS PER YEAR MEAN TEMP. ABOVE 68° F:

- MORE THAN 120
- 90-120
- 60-90
- 30-60
- LESS THAN 30
- AREAS WHERE MEAN DAILY TEMP. DOES NOT EXCEED 68° F

2-6   PRECIPITATION (INCHES), APR-OCT

MAP 36B — WINTER TEMPERATURES AND DURATION OF SNOW COVER

LEGEND   AVERAGE NO. DAYS PER YEAR MEAN TEMP. BELOW 14° F:

- MORE THAN 180
- 150-180
- 120-150
- 90-120
- 60-90
- 30-60
- LESS THAN 30
- AREAS WHERE MEAN DAILY TEMP. NOT LESS THAN 14° F.

60   DURATION OF SNOW COVER IN DAYS

cavalry highway from Mongolia west to Moldavia and beyond Russia into Hungary. Once conquered and pacified by Russia, this region became her granary. The European steppes and the southern fringe of the adjoining mixed forest zone are still the most densely populated general areas in the nation. Elsewhere, equally heavy concentrations are found only in urban regions of the Caucasus, the two capitals, and Central Asia, especially the Fergana Valley.

Much of the steppe is thick, black chernozem, the most fertile soil in the world. Because of this, nearly all of the true steppe zone is now under cultivation. However, the low relative humidity and the small and erratic rainfall which helped to cover 12 per cent of the U.S.S.R. with chernozem also make its cultivation precarious. Much of the area receives only six to twelve inches of rain during the period April-October (see Map 36A), and an entire summer month without rain is not uncommon. This is especially true in the eastern steppes, where the virgin lands have recently been plowed up. Wind erosion is a serious problem in cultivating these drier grasslands.

The last major zone is the million square miles of semi-desert and true desert of Soviet Central Asia. Here the precipitation is scanty, especially in the summer months, and the temperature ranges are great. Summer temperatures are higher than in the tropics; in the southern desert they may reach 122° F. in the shade, and even in the Tashkent area the sand has been recorded at 158° F. Yet winters in the semi-desert are more severe than on the Gulf of Finland; lows of —40° have been recorded. Tashkent, in the true desert zone, has seen —22° F. temperatures, and its snow cover lasts an average of 37 days.

Much of the area is barren sand dune, clay, or rock. Where water is available, however, lush jungle vegetation may occur. The delta of the Amu-Darya even harbors tigers. Under irrigation, the productivity of the fertile desert is great for crops that require much sun and heat. By the utilization of melting waters from snows and glaciers of the nearby mountains, ribbons of steppe-like land in the Fergana Valley have been coverted into one of the world's main cotton-growing regions. Grapes and melons also flourish in such an environment.

The region's economic development is largely a recent achievement. These non-Slavic areas played little role in Russian history prior to the sixteenth century, when their gradual conquest began (see Maps 13, 18, and 25). Even after their complete subjugation in the nineteenth century, their importance was more strategic than economic until the Soviet era. Nature has placed severe limits on the possibilities of even modern technology in this arid zone; population is still centered at the higher elevations and near the old waterways, notably those centers of ancient civilizations, the Amu-Darya and the Syr-Darya Rivers.

There are small zones of subtropical vegetation in the foothills of the Pamir and Tien Shan (Tyan Shan) Mountains, along the southern shore of the Crimea, the western shore of the Caspian, and in the coastal regions of Transcaucasia (see Map 35). Sesame is one of Central Asia's tropical plants, and tea and citrus fruits from Transcaucasia contribute to the relative self-sufficiency of Russia's agriculture.

Map 37. Relief

Historic Implications of Russia's Topography

For all its vastness, Russia is a relatively isolated country. Except in the west, access to her 36,000 miles of frontier is difficult. The Arctic coast and much of the Soviet Far East is locked in oceanic ice for long periods of the year.

Mountains and high plateaus ring most of the southern and eastern borders, from the Carpathians and Causasus in the west to the Anadyr in the extreme northeast (see Map 37). In Asiatic Russia, the border zone includes some of the world's most majestic and inaccessible mountains. The highest in the U.S.S.R. is 24,590-foot Communism Peak, alias Stalin Peak, alias Garmo Peak, in the rugged Pamirs, where numerous other peaks tower to 16–18,000 feet. The Tien Shan Ranges just northeast of the Pamirs also exceed 16,000 feet in places. Continuing northeast, the Inner Altay Mountains reach a maximum of 15,000 feet. Eastward from the adjoining Sayan Mountains, altitudes over 10,000 feet are rare (except for the volcanoes of Kamchatka), but the belt of 5–8,000-foot domes is wide all the way to the Bering Straits. This formidable southern wall helps to explain some of the ethnic differences between the populations of Siberia and the rest of Asia.

The lofty and rugged nature of the Caucasus Mountains partially explains both the heterogeneous population of the dissected region and the difficulties involved in the protracted Russian conquest of the area (see Map 24). The Vodorazdelny Range averages 11,800 feet, and Mt. Elbrus in the even higher Peredovoy Range reaches 18,468 feet.

Excepting ranges in the almost uninhabited lands east of the Lena River, the only important north–south mountains are the Urals, which stretch for 1,500 miles at 60° E. Longitude. However, this traditional but meaningless dividing line between Europe and Asia is narrow in the center, where altitudes seldom exceed 1,300 feet. The highest point is far to the north, at 6,214 feet. The rounded Urals in many respects resemble the Appalachians, and they are no more of a barrier to modern communications than their American counterpart.

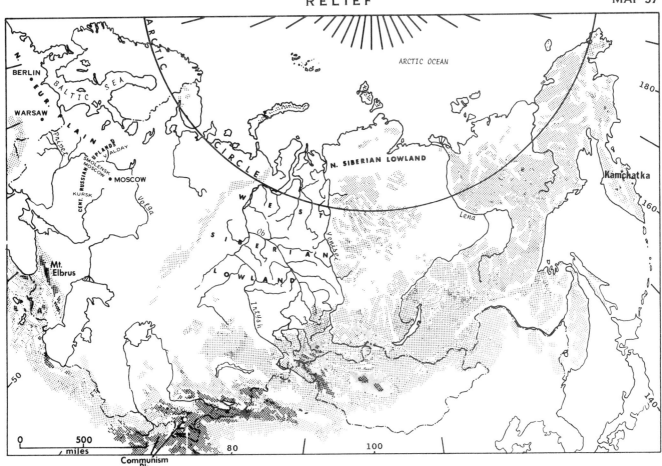

LEGEND

NOTE: RIVERS IN THE WEST SIBERIAN LOWLAND ARE SHOWN IN DISPROPORTIONATE DETAIL.

ELEVATION IN FEET (METERS):

☐ 0-1640 (0-500M) (CASPIAN SHORE BELOW SEA LEVEL)	▨ 1640-6562 (500-2000M)	▧ 6562-9843 (2000-3000M)	▨ 9843-16405 (3000-5000M)	▨ OVER 16405 (OVER 5000M)

The huge West Siberian Lowland, extending some 1,200 miles from the Urals to the Yenisei River and 1,100–1,600 miles from north to south, is one of the most impenetrable and undeveloped areas on earth. Including the Ob and Irtysh rivers and their many sluggish tributaries (depicted in disproportionate detail on Map 37 for emphasis), it is a region of marshes, gigantic spring floods, and exceptionally level terrain. Heights rarely exceed 400 feet, and much of the land is only 15 to 30 feet above the rivers. Similar conditions are found in much of the North Siberian Lowland, which is an extension of this region toward the Lena delta.

West of the Urals, the great European Russian Plain stretches some 1,500 monotonous miles to Poland, where it merges with the Northern European Plain, which continues to the English Channel. Most of European Russia lies below 656 feet; even the Central Russian Uplands (the Valday, Smolensk-Moscow and Kursk hills) are generally under 800 feet, although the Valday Hills reach 1,125 feet at their maximum. Despite their low elevation, these uplands are significant as the watershed of the numerous and historically important rivers of European Russia (compare Maps 7 and 37).

It is not mere coincidence that the exposed western border of Russia is also the one that has witnessed the most violent fluctuations throughout her history. Except for the Pripet (Pripyat) Marshes (and a small corner of the Carpathian Mountains first acquired in 1945), there is no natural obstacle more imposing than a river or small hill between Moscow and Berlin. The wide doorway between the Pripet River and the Baltic has been the scene of countless invasions of Russia. It must be remembered, however, that this door works both ways—the eighteenth, nineteenth, and twentieth centuries have all witnessed Russian armies in Central Europe.

Appendix

Name Changes of Selected Russian Cities and Towns

An exhaustive list of name changes for inhabited places in the U.S.S.R. would fill a large gazetteer. Given the Russian—especially the Soviet—propensity for changing designations for political reasons, even this modest list may become partially obsolete before the ink is dry. Regardless of future additions, however, a record of past changes is useful to the historian.

Except for a few unusually interesting cases (e.g. Akkerman), the sequences of non-Russian designations for places later annexed by Russia are omitted. In general, only places whose Russian names have changed are included; exceptions are cities which were abandoned during the period of Russia's history (e.g. Sarkel). Locations are included only for names that apply to more than one place, where confusion is likely.

Arrangement

Entries are arranged alphabetically with cross-references to the earliest name listed for each place. Earliest name entries include all subsequent listed changes, with dates for each change in parentheses. Earliest name entries also include accent marks, for all listed changes, as a guide to pronunciation. (N.B.: Russian words are accented on only one syllable. The letter *e* with an umlaut *(ë)* is pronounced *yo* and is stressed. The umlaut is not used in Russian spelling.)

Abbreviations Used with Dates

c. — circa (approximate date)
C — century
f. — founded, first mentioned, or first settled (not necessarily as a town; many towns originated as tiny frontier forts, monasteries, or economic enterprises)
R. — date of Russian occupation and/or annexation.

Akkermán (site of ancient Greek Tyras; possession varied until Turks captured it in 1484 and named it A.; R. 1812)—Bélgorod-Dnestróvski (1944)

Ak-Mechét (f.c. 1820)—Peróvsk (R. 1853)—Kzyl-Ordá (c. 1924)

Akmólinsk (f. 1824)—Tselinográd (1961)

Alchévsk (f. 1895)—Voroshílovsk (1931)—Kommunársk (1959)

Aleksandrópol (f. 1834 on site of ancient Gumri)—Leninakán (1924)

Aleksándrovsk (f. 1770)—Zaporózhe (1921)

Aleksandrovski. See Gusevka

Alma-Ata. See Verny

Arkhangelsk. See Novo-Kholmogory

Artemovsk. See Bakhmut

Ashkhabad. See Askhabad

Askhabád (f. 1881)—Poltorátsk (1919) —Ashkhabád (1927)

Aulie-Ata. See Taraz

Bakhmút (f.c. 1571)—Artëmovsk (1924)

Belaya Vezha. See Sarkel

Belgorod-Dnestrovski. See Akkerman

Beloózero (f.c. 862)—Belozérsk (due to plague, town moved 10 mi. w. at end of 14th C; later took present name)

Belozersk. See Beloozero

Berdyánsk (f. 1827)—Osipénko (1939) —Berdyánsk (1958)

Bereste (f. before 1017)—Brest-Litóvsk (1340; acquired by Lithuania c. 1319; regained by Rus. 1795)—Brest (c. 1921)

Blagoveshchensk (on Amur). See Ust-Zeyski

Bóbriki (f. 1930)—Stalinogórsk (1934) —Novomoskóvsk (1961)

Bogoródsk (f. 1781)—Nogínsk (1930)

Bólgar (Bulgar, on Volga; f. 10th C or earlier; virtually destroyed by Mongols in 1237)—Bólgar Velíki (1399; regained importance after 1280s; destroyed by Russians in 1431)

Bolgar Veliki. See Bolgar

Brest. See Bereste

Brest-Litovsk. See Bereste

Bukhará (f. before 5th C; R. 1868)— Stáraya Bukhará (c. 1888)—Bukhará (1935)

Chkalov. See Orenburg

Daugavpils. See Dinaburg

Derpt. See Yurev

Detskoe Selo. See Tsarskoe Selo

Dínaburg (Dünaburg, f. 1278; R. 1772) —Dvinsk (1893)—Dáugavpils (1917)

Dneprodzerzhinsk. See Kamenskoe

Dnepropetrovsk. See Ekaterinoslav

Donetsk. See Yuzovka

Dushanbe. See Dyushambe

Dvinsk. See Dinaburg

Dyushambé (small village destroyed 1922; rebuilt after 1923)—Stalinabád (1929)—Dushanbé (1961)

Dzaudzhikau. See Vladikavkaz

Dzerzhinsk (on Oka, near Gorki). See Rastyapino

Dzerzhinsk (in Ukraine). See Shcherbinovka

Dzhambul. See Taraz

Egoshikha (f.c. early 17th C)—Perm (1781)—Mólotov (1940)—Perm (1957)

Ekaterinbúrg (f. 1721)—Sverdlóvsk (1924)

Ekaterinodár (f. 1794)—Krasnodár (1920)

Ekaterinosláv (f.c. 1783)—Novorossísk (late 18th C)—Ekaterinosláv (1802) —Dnepropetróvsk (1926)

Elisavetpol. See Gandzha

Elizavetgrád (f.c. 1754)—Zinóvevsk (1924)—Kírovo (c. 1934)—Kirovográd (1939)

Fergana. See Novy Margelan

Frunze. See Pishpek

Gagarin. See Gzhatsk

Gandzhá (f.c. 5th C)—Elisavetpól (R. 1804)—Gandzhá (1918)—Kirovabád (1935)

Gorki. *See* Nizhni Novgorod

Gorodéts Meshchérski (f.c. 1152)—Kasímov (1471)

Gusevka (f. 1893)—Aleksándrovski (1894)—Novonikoláevsk (1895)—Novosibírsk (c. 1925)

Gzhatsk (f. 1719)—Gagárin (1968)

Itíl (f.c. 8th C; destroyed c. 967; site 10 mi. upstream from present city Astrakhán)

Ivánovo (f. before 1561)—Ivánovo-Voznesénsk (1871)—Ivánovo (1932)

Ivanovo-Voznesensk. *See* Ivanovo

Kagan. *See* Novaya Bukhara

Kalinin. *See* Tver

Kaliningrad. *See* Kënigsberg

Kámenskoe (f. mid-18th C)—Dneprodzerzhínsk (1936)

Kashlyk. *See* Sibir

Kasimov. *See* Gorodets Meshcherski

Kënigsberg (f. 1255; R. 1945)—Kaliningrád (1946)

Khlýnov (f.c. 1174)—Vyátka (c. 1780)—Kírov (1934)

Khodzhént (f. 8th C or earlier; R. 1866)—Leninabád (1936)

Khrushchëv (f. 1954 but named 1961)—Krémges (1962)—Svetlovódsk (1969)

Kirov. *See* Khlynov

Kirovabad. *See* Gandzha

Kirovo. *See* Elizavetgrad

Kirovograd. *See* Elizavetgrad

Kommunarsk. *See* Alchevsk

Krasnodar. *See* Ekaterinodar

Kremges. *See* Khrushchev

Kuybyshev (on Volga). *See* Samara

Kuznétsk (on Trans-Sib. R.R.; f. 1617)—Stálinsk (1932)—Nóvokuznétsk (1961)

Kzyl-Orda. *See* Ak-Mechet

Leninabad. *See* Khodzhent

Leninakan. *See* Aleksandropol

Leningrad. *See* Saint Petersburg

Leninogorsk (Kazakh S.S.R.). *See* Ridder

Lugánsk (f.c. 1795 as factory settlement; named L. 1882)—Voroshilovgrád (1935)—Lugánsk (1958)

Makhachkala. *See* Petrovsk

Mariúpol (f. 1779)—Zhdánov (1948)

Mary. *See* Merv

Merv (f. 1824, 19 mi. w. of ancient [4th C B.C. or earlier] Merv, which was abandoned soon after; R. 1884)—Marý (1937)

Mirzoyan. *See* Taraz

Molotov. *See* Egoshikha

Mólotovsk (at mouth of N. Dvina, village Sudostrói renamed M. in 1938)—Severodvínsk (1957)

Molotovsk (s. of Kirov). *See* Nolinsk

Nadézhdinsk (f. 1894)—Sérov (1939)

Nikoláevsk (18th C village, took name N. in 1835)—Pugachëv (1918)

Nikólsk-Ussuríyski (formed 1898 by merger of Nikolskoe and another village)—Voroshílov (1935)—Ussuríysk (1957)

Nízhni Nóvgorod (f. 1221)—Górki (1932)

Noginsk. *See* Bogorodsk

Nólinsk (f. 1780)—Mólotovsk (1940)—Nólinsk (1958)

Nóvaya Bukhará (f. 1888 as R.R. Sta. for Bukhara)—Kagán (1935)

Nóvo-Kholmogóry (f. 1584)—Arkhángelsk (1613)

Novokuznetsk. *See* Kuznetsk

Novomoskovsk. *See* Bobriki

Novonikolaevsk. *See* Gusevka

Novorossisk (on Dnieper). *See* Ekaterinoslav

Novosibirsk. *See* Gusevka

Nóvy Margelán (f. 1876)—Skóbelev (1907)—Ferganá (1924)

Novy Saray. *See* Saray

Obdórsk (f. 1595)—Salekhárd (1933)

Ordzhonikidze (on Terek). *See* Vladi-kavkaz

Orenbúrg (f. 1735 near present Orsk; moved 1743 to new site; a garrison remained at future city Orsk)—Chkálov (1938)—Orenbúrg (1957)

Osipenko. *See* Berdyansk

Perm. *See* Egoshikha

Perovsk. *See* Ak-Mechet

Petrograd. *See* Saint Petersburg

Petróvsk (f. 1844)—Petróvsk-Port (1857)—Makhachkalá (1921)

Petróvski Zavód (f. 1789)—Petróvsk-Zabaykálski (1926)

Petrovsk-Port. *See* Petrovsk

Petrovsk-Zabaykalski. *See* Petrovski Zavod

Pishpék (f. 1825; R. 1862)—Frúnze (1926)

Poltoratsk. *See* Askhabad

Pugachev. *See* Nikolaevsk

Pushkin. *See* Tsarskoe Selo

Rastyápino (summer colony Chernoreche became workers' settlement Rastyapino c. 1918)—Dzerzhínsk (1929)

Rídder (f. 1794)—Leninogórsk (c. 1939)

Rybánsk (f.c. 1137)—Rýbnaya Slobodá (15th C)—Rýbinsk (1777)—Shcherbakóv (1946)—Rýbinsk (1957)

Rybinsk. *See* Rybansk

Rybnaya Sloboda. *See* Rybansk

Saint Petersburg (Sankt-Peterbúrg, f. 1703)—Petrográd (1914)—Leningrád (1924)

Salekhard. *See* Obdorsk

Samára (f. 1586)—Kúybyshev (1935)

Saráy (f.c. 1240s by Khan Batu near Volga delta; during reign of Berke [c. 1257–66] another S. was founded upstream where the Volga is closer to the Don. This New (Nóvy) S. became the capital of the Golden Horde during the reign of Uzbek [c. 1312–41], when Old [Stáry] S. was abandoned. New Saray was virtually destroyed by Tamerlane in 1395, finally destroyed in 1502 by Crimean Tartars)

Sarkél (f.c. 834)—Bélaya Vézha (R.c. 965; abandoned c. 1117)

Sérgiev (f. as Tróitse-Sérgieva Lávra [monastery] c. 1337)—Zagórsk (1930)

Serov. *See* Nadezhdinsk

Severodvinsk. *See* Molotovsk

Shcherbakov. *See* Rybansk

Shcherbínovka (f. 1860)—Dzerzhínsk (1938)

Sibír (f. 14th C or earlier)—Kashlýk (R. 1582; abandoned c. 1587 when Tobolsk founded 10 mi. downstream)

Simbírsk (f. 1648)—Ulyánovsk (1924)

Skobelev. *See* Novy Margelan

Sovetsk. *See* Tilzit

Stalinabad. *See* Dyushambe

Stalingrad. *See* Tsaritsyn

Stalino (in Ukraine). *See* Yuzovka

Stalinogorsk. *See* Bobriki

Stalinsk. *See* Kuznetsk

Staraya Bukhara. *See* Bukhara

Stary Saray. *See* Saray

Stávropol (N. Caucasus, f. 1777)—Voroshílovsk (c. 1935)—Stávropol (1943)

Stávropol (on Volga, small town moved to present site in 1955 due to dam construction)—Tolyátti (renamed for Togliatti in 1964)

Sverdlovsk (in Urals). *See* Ekaterinburg

Svetlovodsk. *See* Khrushchev

Taráz (Talás, f.c. 7th C; destroyed by Mongols in 13th C)—Aulié-Atá (f. late 18th C, R. 1864)—Mirzoyán (c. 1936)—Dzhambúl (c. 1938)

Tartu. *See* Yurev

Tbilísi (f. 4th C, R. 1801)—Tiflís (1801)—Tbilísi (1936)

Tiflis. *See* Tbilisi

Tilzít (Tilsit, f. 1288; R. 1945)—Sovétsk (1946)

Tolyatti. *See* Stavropol

Tsarítsyn (f. 1589)—Stalingrád (1925)—Volgográd (1961)

Tsárskoe Seló (f. 1718 at site of Finnish village seized c. 1708)—Détskoe Seló (c. 1917)—Púshkin (1937)

Tselinograd. *See* Akmolinsk

Tver (f.c. 12th C)—Kalínin (1931)

Údinsk (f. 1666)—Verkhneúdinsk (1689)—Ulán-Udé (1934)

Ulan-Ude. *See* Udinsk

Ulyanovsk. *See* Simbirsk

Uralsk. *See* Yaitski Gorodok

Ussuriysk. *See* Nikolsk-Ussuriyski

Ust-Zéyski (f. 1856)—Blagovéshchensk (1858)

Verkhneudinsk. *See* Udinsk

Vérny (f. 1854 on site of Kazakh settlement Almata)—Almá-Atá (1921)

Vladikavkáz (f. 1784)—Ordzhonikídze (1932)—Dzaudzhikáu (1944)—Ordzhonikídze (1954)

Volgograd. *See* Tsaritsyn

Voroshilov. *See* Nikolsk-Ussuriyski

Voroshilovgrad. *See* Lugansk

Voroshilovsk (in Ukraine). *See* Alchevsk

Voroshilovsk (N. Caucasus). *See* Stavropol

Vyatka. *See* Khlynov

Yaítski Gorodók (on middle Ural River; f. 1613)—Urálsk (1775)

Yúrev (f.c. 1030 at site of 10th C village Tarpatu)—Derpt (Rus. for Ger. Dorpat, seized by Germans in 1224; R. [regained] 1704)—Yúrev (1893)—Tártu (1918)

Yúzovka (f. 1869)—Stálino (1924)—Donétsk (1961)

Zagorsk. *See* Sergiev

Zaporozhe. *See* Aleksandrovsk

Zhdanov. *See* Mariupol

Zinovevsk. *See* Elizavetgrad